Grassland & Woodland in Summer

Reader's Digest
Wildlife Watch

Grassland & Woodland in Summer

Published by
The Reader's Digest Association Limited
London • New York • Sydney • Montreal

Contents

Wildlife habitats and havens

12 Wildlife of arable farmland

18 Roadside verges

22 Life in an old apple orchard

28 Hazel coppice

34 The Chilterns

Woodland watch

84 The roe deer

90 The common dormouse

94 The redstart

98 The bullfinch

102 Recognising small warblers

105 The purple emperor

107 The stag beetle

109 Blood-red ants

111 Recognising smaller deciduous trees

116 Forget-me-nots

121 Climbers and scramblers

126 Index

128 Acknowledgments

Animals and plants in focus

Grassland watch

40 The common shrew

46 The field vole

52 The skylark

58 The lapwing

64 Burnet moths

66 Recognising downland butterflies

71 The glow-worm

73 Poppies

78 Clovers

Introduction

Summer begins in June, at that most enchanting of times when the pale sunlight of spring ripens into a rich, golden glow that permeates the landscape like warm honey. On rolling chalklands and limestone hills the warmth can seem almost audible as innumerable grasshoppers keep up a constant, fervent buzz of song in the long grass.

Stirred into action by the heat, grassland orchids push their flowering spikes up into the sunlight, some displaying vivid splashes of colour. One such is the pyramidal orchid, with pinkish red spires that are conical at first but become rounder as summer progresses. Others have an air of muted mystery, such as the elusive bee orchid, which resembles a bumblebee landing on a flower. The land even smells warm, as wild flowers scent the air and mown hay meadows in the valleys release an exquisite fragrance of sweet vernal grass.

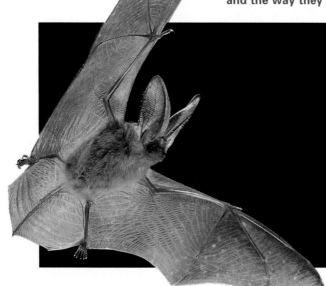

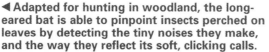

◄ Adapted for hunting in woodland, the long-eared bat is able to pinpoint insects perched on leaves by detecting the tiny noises they make, and the way they reflect its soft, clicking calls.

▲ Usually to be seen feeding on bramble flowers in woodland clearings, the white admiral breeds on the long honeysuckle vines that trail from the trees. The adults appear for just a few weeks in summer.

▲ July is the peak flowering time for the ox-eye daisy, which often forms spectacular drifts on road verges, along the edges of arable fields and in uncut hay meadows. The flowers are a valuable source of nectar for insects.

Butterfly banks

Until recently vast tracts of native grassland survived on the chalk downlands of the south, but much of it has now been ploughed under in order to grow barley and other crops. The fragments that remain on steep slopes or in remote hollows and valleys are precious refuges for wildlife. Their complex, interwoven tapestry of plant life has developed over centuries, with the taller, more vigorous species suppressed by the nibbling teeth of sheep or rabbits. This allows orchids to flourish, along with other low-growing plants, such as vetches and trefoils, silverweed and speedwells.

Such plants are vital to the downland butterflies that flutter among the grasses (see pages 66–70). Although the adults will sip sweet nectar from virtually any type of flower, they are very choosy about the plants on which they lay their eggs, because their caterpillars will eat only certain species. For instance, the Adonis blue – the males of which are a stunning iridescent azure – lays its eggs on horseshoe vetch, and then only on plants that are growing in short turf on sunny, south-facing banks. For protection from predators, the caterpillars rely on ants that dot the ancient chalkland turf with their anthills, supplying these industrious creatures in turn with sweet honeydew. Perhaps not surprisingly, the Adonis blue has always been scarce, but it has become increasingly rare as ancient native grasslands have been replaced with arable crops. Some of the best places to find this butterfly are on the grassy ramparts of the prehistoric hillforts that crown the southern downs – places such as Maiden Castle in Dorset, where the flower-rich turf has survived for more than 2000 years.

Coastal glory

In the far north a similar type of grassland has developed in a very different place – the Atlantic coasts of the Outer Hebrides. Here, white sand enriched by the chalky remains of pulverised seashells has been swept inland by the wind, to form the basis of a coastal strip of grassland known as the machair. By mid-June this has turned to a sea of flowers as a glorious variety of plants bursts into bloom. They include many chalk and limestone species that flourish on the lime-rich soil, including the vetches, trefoils

▲ In summer many ragwort plants are stripped bare by caterpillars of the striped cinnabar moth. The caterpillars concentrate poisons from the plants in their bodies and so become poisonous in their turn.

▼ The shaggy cap of the parasol mushroom can grow to 30cm (12in) or more across. It often appears on grassland in late summer, when the weather is warm but wet – ideal mushroom-growing conditions.

▶ The Hebridean machair is one of the few places in Britain where the corncrake still breeds. Its scientific name, *Crex crex*, is a perfect description of the male's rasping call.

and clovers (see pages 78–82) that grow on downland far to the south. In some places, 220 different plant species have been found growing together.

The dazzling flora of the machair is not entirely natural, however. As on the sheep-grazed turf of the chalklands, it is the result of centuries of selective cropping that favours some types of plants at the expense of others. The most productive parts of the region are those stretches that have been used to grow hay crops, harvested in July after the plants have flowered and set seed. This strategy has enabled delicate grassland plants to multiply while preventing the growth of bigger plants that would otherwise overwhelm the flowers.

Country birds

This land management also favours the birds that nest on the machair, since by the time the mower arrives the young have already fledged. These birds include the corncrake – now virtually extinct in mainland Britain – as well as the far more widespread, but declining, skylark and lapwing (see pages 52–63).

Birds such as these are typical of open countryside and often nest on cultivated land. Other than on the machair, they have suffered in recent decades as the traditional late hay crop has been replaced by an earlier harvest of green grass to make silage, at a time when the birds are still nesting.

Skylarks and lapwings are also badly affected by the planting of winter crops and, like all the wildlife of arable farmland (see pages 12–17), are scarce on land where intensive methods are used. The absence of fallow fields over winter makes insects and other food hard to find, and by spring autumn-sown crops are too dense for birds to nest among them.

Fortunately, on a few farms the older-style mixed farming is still practised, and their fields can be a joy to see in summer, fringed by drifts of plants that some people regard as weeds, such as cornflower, mayweed and poppy (see pages 73–77), with yellowhammers singing in the hedges and skylarks overhead.

Green shade

Most of the grasslands and fields of Britain were once woodland, and in places where old pastures are no longer heavily grazed, encroaching scrub is gradually turning them back into woodland again.

Here the skylark's song is replaced by the harsh calls and scratchy warbling of the common whitethroat and the silvery notes of the willow warbler (see pages 102–104), both more typical of the woodland edge than open countryside.

▲ The yellow rattle gets its name from the sound ripe seeds make inside its dry capsules in August. Unusually, this common grassland plant obtains some of its nutrients by tapping into the food supply of other plants, so it is semi-parasitic.

◄ Although the mole spends most of its time underground in the network of tunnels that it digs beneath old pasture, it will occasionally surface to feed on earthworms.

▲ A spring and summer visitor from Africa, the pied flycatcher breeds mainly in open oak woodland, where it can be seen darting in and out of the canopy foliage in pursuit of flying insects.

Within the woods themselves, the birds are less vocal than they were in spring, but many are still busy feeding second broods of young. They can be hard to see among the heavy foliage of the canopy, but patience may be rewarded by a glimpse of a foraging treecreeper or – especially in western oakwoods – a pied flycatcher or redstart (see pages 94–97). The summer canopy is at its thickest in beechwoods, such as those in the Chilterns (see pages 34–37), casting a green shade that suppresses undergrowth, leaving the woodland floor almost bare except for a carpet of last autumn's fallen leaves. This creates a wonderfully atmospheric effect, but bird and insect life is scarce because there is relatively little to eat.

Woodland animals are more in evidence at the edges of clearings, such as those made by coppicing, an ancient system of woodland management that is now being revived as a conservation technique. It involves harvesting the top growth of trees, especially hazel (see pages 28–33), to make more shoots grow, which can then be harvested in turn. This allows more light to reach the woodland floor, encouraging low-growing plants that do not like shade. The flowers provide nectar for bees, hoverflies and woodland butterflies, such as the speckled wood and the magnificent silver-washed

fritillary. In July and August, sweet sap bleeding from newly cut hazel stumps may even lure the elusive purple emperor down towards ground level – a species that spends most of its time flying high up among the tree tops (see pages 105–106). The insects are sought out by birds, and as the bramble scrub flourishes and new hazel shoots appear, their foliage attracts browsing roe deer (see pages 84–89).

Late harvest

By September the brambles are covered with blackberries, providing a feast for blackbirds, thrushes, whitethroats, blackcaps and bullfinches (see pages 98–101), as well as wood mice and even foxes. Meanwhile, hazel nuts from mature trees are gathered and eaten by dormice (see pages 90–93) and by grey squirrels. For all these creatures, the fruitfulness of late summer is a sign that autumn and winter are coming, and that they need to build up their energy reserves. Some need the food to keep them alive during hibernation. Others, such as the redstart, need it to fuel their long migration to warmer regions. By the end of September many of these migrants will have gone, leaving the residents to face the falling temperatures and strengthening winds of autumn.

▲ A plant of chalk grassland, the bee orchid is scarce and easily missed, despite its distinctive, insect-like flowers, which appear in June and July.

▲ The massive bill of the hawfinch is strong enough to crack cherry stones and other hard-cased seeds, which it finds mainly in mixed woodland. In summer, it tends to forage high in the trees, and is usually difficult to see.

▶ Late summer fruits provide vital food for the wood mouse, as it builds up its fat reserves in preparation for winter. Unlike some other small mammals, such as the dormouse, it stays active throughout the year.

Wildlife habitats and havens

- Wildlife of arable farmland
- Roadside verges
- Life in an old apple orchard
- A hazel coppice
- The Chilterns

Wildlife of arable farmland

Wild flowers edge fields of ripening grain with splashes of scarlet and blue, while tangled hedgerows and hidden wild corners draw birds, mice and voles to the cultivated land.

Farmland is at its most attractive in summer, when the bare earth of arable fields is hidden beneath growing crops, and wheat, barley and other cereals are ripening to gold under the summer sun. Field edges are often bright with wild flowers such as poppies and corn marigolds. Farmland birds, such as skylarks and meadow pipits, sing overhead, and when the harvest starts the air is filled with the distinctive aroma of grain. Such sights, sounds and scents are still to be enjoyed in many parts of

Britain, despite increasingly intensive farming techniques that have changed the nature of British agriculture over the past few decades.

There are two basic types of farmland – pasture and arable. Pasture consists of grass grown for grazing animals, such as cattle and sheep, while arable is cultivated land used to grow crops for harvesting. Traditionally, two major types of crops predominated – cereals and root crops. Today, the variety of crops that are farmed is enormous. Oil seeds are widely grown, with rape

and linseed colouring whole fields vivid yellow and ethereal blue respectively when they flower. Many farmers also raise crops for animal feed, such as field beans, maize and stubble turnips. On the rich soils of the East Anglian Fens, for example, vast areas are devoted to cash crops such as sugar beet, peas for the frozen-food trade, potatoes and leeks.

All crops represent a big investment of time and resources, and the livelihood of the farmer depends on achieving a good return on the investment. So arable

fields have always been treated more like factory production lines rather than wildlife habitats. As far as possible, competing plants – or weeds – and plant-eating animals have been controlled or excluded. For thousands of years the methods used were relatively inefficient, and this enabled a wide variety of wildlife to thrive on arable land.

A century ago each crop attracted its own varied population of plants and insects. Until 40 or 50 years ago most cereal crops were bright red with poppies in

► Along field edges and in unmanaged corners that have been left to lie fallow, native wild flowers flourish, including dandelions, poppies and cornflowers.

▲ Arable fields are colonised afresh each year by the harvest mouse. Gathering in the crop destroys the nests of these tiny creatures, so they return from nearby grassland each spring to rebuild them.

► The lapwing favours mixed farmland for breeding, where it can nest in bare, spring-tilled arable fields or short, cattle-grazed grassland.

early summer. When crops were harvested, rich layers of low-growing plants, such as the field pansy, were revealed, and since harvesting methods were less efficient the stubble fields were a source of rich pickings. Many birds relied on the spilt grain and weed seeds to see them through the winter, and local people turned out to glean any grain that had been missed.

Arable monocultures

Modern methods of weed and pest control have changed all this, however. Chemical sprays now make it possible to grow arable crops as pest-free monocultures, in which all weeds are eliminated. This reduces the variety of insects that are able to live on the plants – assuming they are not killed by insecticides – and, in turn, the food available to birds. A wheat field, for instance, provides food for seed-eating birds for just a short time in summer when the grains are soft and milky.

The use of artificial fertilisers has increased crop yields tremendously, but they have had a more far-reaching effect on farmland wildlife. In the past most farmers obtained manure from their livestock. They practised crop rotations that allowed long fallow periods when animals were kept on the land. Since the advent of chemical fertilisers this is no longer necessary, and many farmers grow the same crops year after year, with no breaks. They also plant more crops in autumn so they get bigger yields the following summer, rather than leaving the stubble fields over the winter and planting them in spring.

Colourful survivals

Despite this, remnants of the old farming landscape can still be seen. Many of the weeds of arable farmland produce huge numbers of seeds, which remain viable for many years. When a modern field is not sprayed correctly, or at all, the

Unsprayed strips on the edges of arable fields often develop dazzling shows of flowers such as poppies, and support many insects and birds.

red poppies that grow and flower may be from seeds dropped 10, 20 or even 30 years ago. The same is true of cornflowers, which still flourish on field edges.

One factor that has helped wildlife survive on arable farmland is the interest of the farming community in country sports. Surprising though it may seem, activities such as hunting, shooting and fishing have all helped conserve many wildlife refuges in intensively farmed landscapes. In many areas, almost all the surviving small woods have been retained because they provide cover for

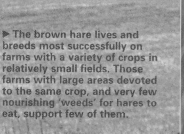

▶ The brown hare lives and breeds most successfully on farms with a variety of crops in relatively small fields. Those farms with large areas devoted to the same crop, and very few nourishing 'weeds' for hares to eat, support few of them.

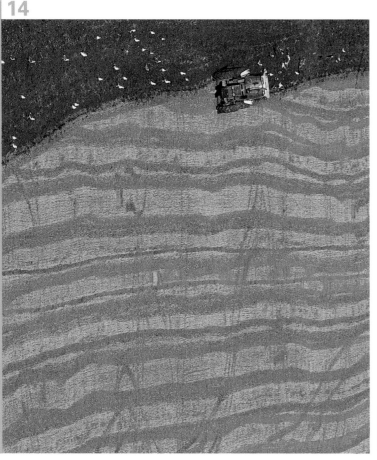

The most familiar arable crops are cereals such as wheat and barley, which are both very important, and the less widely grown oats and rye. Increasingly, farmers are planting valuable oil crops, such as rape and linseed.

Important root crops include potatoes and sugar beet, and the various types of mangels and turnips that are grown as animal feed. Maize is also widely grown, mainly to make silage to feed animals. Several garden crops, such as carrots and peas, are grown on a field scale to supply supermarkets and the frozen-food industry.

▲ Barley is grown for animal feed and to make malt for brewing.

▶ Turnips were probably first grown in Britain by the Romans. They are fed to sheep in winter.

◀ Maize used to be grown only for animal feed, but new varieties are sold as sweetcorn.

▲ Gulls often move inland to feed. They soon spot a tractor ploughing the fields and fly down to follow it closely in the hope of seizing worms and insects from the newly turned soil.

▶ Common, black-headed and herring gulls have all developed the habit of feeding on arable land.

foxes and pheasants. Hunting was also the reason for retaining hedges that might otherwise have been grubbed out, because one of the main attractions of the hunt was the opportunity it provided for jumping hedges on horseback. In the past, hunting farmers planned whole landscapes with this in mind. Since February 2005, however, hunting with hounds has been illegal, and some of these fox coverts and hedged landscapes may disappear as a result.

Shooting, however, remains legal, and this encourages farmers to retain hedges and rough corners for nesting pheasants and partridges. The ends of fields are often left unsprayed as 'conservation headlands' to encourage gamebirds, and these provide

habitats for scarce native plants as well as food and shelter for insects, birds, small mammals and other wildlife.

Boundary refuges

On many tracts of arable farmland all the wildlife interest is concentrated in the field boundaries. These vary in style around the country, from the ditches and dykes of the Fens, to the stone walls of the northern Dales and the ancient hedges and hedgerow trees of Devon. In many areas these boundaries date back centuries or even millennia,

and still retain traces of the wild habitat that existed before the land was farmed.

In the Fens, vegetation growing alongside ditches may contain breeding birds such as skylarks, meadow pipits and reed buntings, while mallard and even little grebes may be found swimming on the ditch water. In other places, the densest hedges may have many small birds nesting in them, and species such as kestrels, little owls and barn owls may breed in holes in hedgerow trees and hunt over the farmland. A much scarcer,

but now increasing, species is the hobby. This small, elegant falcon spends the winter in sub-Saharan Africa and migrates to Britain in May. It breeds late and feeds on large insects and small birds.

Threatened birds

Unfortunately, many hedges have been destroyed over the last 50 years, because bigger farm machines have made large fields more cost-effective. Combined with the effects of pesticides and the increase in autumn planting, which reduces feeding opportunities on winter stubbles, this has had a disastrous effect on the wildlife of farmland. Most farmland birds are under threat to some degree, but those that breed on arable land show declines over the widest range of species. The flocks of lapwings that used to be common on many fields have been seriously reduced and few now breed on arable land. One sight that is still common, however, is a crowd of gulls following the plough, for the turning of the soil stirs up plenty of worms, insect grubs and other animals for the gulls to eat.

KEY BIRDS OF ARABLE FARMLAND

A number of birds are more likely to be found on and around cultivated farmland than in any other habitat. The corn bunting is one of these. It is a dumpy brown bird resembling a female house sparrow, although somewhat bigger. The males have a curious trilling song that is often compared to the jangle of a bunch of keys. Although the song sounds simple it is actually very complex, with local differences that persist for years. The males are among the most sexually active of songbirds – many have two mates, and harems of three or four females are not unusual.

The record is 18 in a single season. Despite its sexual energy, the corn bunting is extinct in many areas where it used to nest, and numbers are seriously reduced in other regions. Loss of vital insect food during the breeding season may be one reason for its decline, for like most seed-eating birds it feeds its young on insects to ensure they get enough protein. The almost universal use of pesticides has eliminated most insects from arable land, and the corn bunting is suffering as a result.

The related cirl bunting is also in decline, reduced to about 700 pairs, which inhabit a small area of south Devon. The Royal Society for the Protection of Birds (RSPB) is trying to reverse this trend by encouraging farmers to leave winter stubbles, where the birds can find weed seeds, and also hedges, because these are full of insects in summer.

The stone curlew is a crow-sized wader that favours habitats with free-draining, stony soils. In Britain it is a bird of south-western downland, particularly Salisbury Plain and Porton Down, and the grass heaths of the East Anglian Breckland. With the loss of much of this favoured habitat, it has been forced increasingly to breed on adjacent arable land, where it often nests among spring-sown crops such as carrots and kale. It has an eerie, penetrating call, which is mostly uttered at night. It also forages for food at night, its large eyes enabling it to see in the gloom. The stone curlews that breed in Britain winter in Spain, south-west France and north Africa. There are currently more than 300 breeding pairs.

▲ Cirl buntings are sparrow-sized birds related to yellowhammers. They are among the most threatened of all British birds.

◄ A bulky body, large head, stout bill and streaky plumage characterise the corn bunting. Once abundant on farmland, these birds have become very scarce in recent years.

► The curious stone curlew is well adapted for life in open landscapes, and the birds frequently nest among recently planted crops and on freshly ploughed fields.

On some modern arable farms only a few trees remain to punctuate the virtual monopoly of the cash crop.

Many mammals and birds were valued in the past as hunting quarry, and some are still specially reared to be shot as game. Hunting and shooting often occurred – and sometimes still do – on arable farmland, and these activities have influenced the way in which the land is managed. In particular, many arable farmers derive income from renting shooting rights, and this encourages them to provide semi-wild habitats for gamebirds that also benefit native wildlife.

Fox hunting in its traditional form is now illegal, but foxes are still regularly shot in an effort to reduce fox predation on domestic poultry and other livestock. Since wolves became extinct more than 300 years ago – mainly because of hunting – the fox is Britain's only wild canine. Over much of Britain foxes are thriving, probably because they are very adaptable feeders. In autumn, for example, they may eat fruit, and throughout the year they scavenge carcasses of animals that have been killed on roads. They often travel long distances each night, and in the process they, too, are often killed on roads. Such casualties far outweigh the number that are shot, or were killed by hounds when such hunting was legal.

The pheasant is the classic gamebird, introduced from Asia but now one of the most common of farmland birds. Many breed wild, but millions are released from artificial rearing pens every year to face the guns of shooting parties. In the past, the gamekeepers who reared the

▲ The fox has been pursued for centuries, and in country areas, large numbers are still shot to prevent them killing livestock. Traditionally rural animals, foxes are now numerous in town suburbs, and even in the centres of large cities, where they scavenge for food and have few natural enemies.

◄ Its exotic origins are evident in the cock pheasant's colourful plumage. Pheasants are a common sight on arable farmland all over Britain – and being both numerous and bold they are easy to spot.

▲ Red-legged partridges nest in hedges and around arable field margins.

◄ The grey partridge is less common in most parts of Britain than the red-legged species.

birds killed huge numbers of predators, including species that are now protected, such as rare birds of prey. They still kill stoats, weasels, rats, foxes, crows and magpies, but this style of management is steadily declining, and the mosaic of woodlands, hedges and fields that go to make a good pheasant shoot can be beneficial to other wildlife.

The grey partridge is a native species, unlike the pheasant. Grey partridges live in family parties called coveys during the winter, and burst out of cover as a group when disturbed by the beaters during a partridge shoot. They need good hedges with well-vegetated hedge bottoms for nesting. To raise their young they must have access to semi-wild grassland with plenty of insects.

Introduced from farther south in Europe, the red-legged partridge has adapted

well to arable land over most of England. Its spread has been helped by the fact that it can breed prolifically, given the right conditions, as the female will lay two clutches of eggs – looking after one herself and leaving the other to her mate. Until recently, many reared and released partridges were hybrids of the red-legged partridge and another species, the chukar, but the release of these hybrids has been illegal since 1992.

The hare was also widely hunted in the past, and it is still shot. In most parts of the country it has become rare although there are plenty of areas where it is still common. Hare coursing with dogs is now illegal, but it remains to be seen whether this will boost the hare population, or simply lead to an increase in the numbers that are shot.

Farming for wildlife

A few birds have increased in numbers since intensive farming practices have become widespread. However, these are mainly the bigger common species, such as crows and woodpigeons, that scavenge creatures killed on roads or feed on arable crops. To combat the dangers faced by most rural animals and plants some regions have been designated as Environmentally Sensitive Areas (ESAs), where farmers can receive payments if they manage the land especially for wildlife.

A similar measure is the Countryside Stewardship scheme, under which the farmer is paid to maintain small areas of land for nature conservation and for the value of the landscape. Grants can also be obtained to maintain hedges. On a smaller scale, beetle banks are strips of rough grass left in large fields. They are particularly useful for birds and insects, and provide a refuge for predatory beetles that help the farmer by keeping pest numbers down. The 'conservation headlands' left unsprayed at the edges of fields have a similar value.

Another measure that helps wildlife is set-aside, a scheme imposed on farmers as a way of reducing crop surpluses. Fields are left uncultivated and unsprayed for a year, and many species are able to take advantage of the food and shelter they provide, including seed-eating birds in winter and ground-nesting birds, such as skylarks, in the breeding season. So although farmland wildlife is generally declining, steps are being taken to improve the situation and there is hope for the future.

▲ The barn owl hunts at night over arable farmland. It depends on small mammals for food and as these have declined, so the barn owl has reduced in numbers. Many owls are also killed on the roads at night.

◄ Once common among farm crops, the corncockle is now a rare plant, although its reddish purple flowers can still occasionally be seen from June to August.

▼ Even on vast treeless acres of farmland, with few or no hedgerows, unsprayed field boundaries may attract insects, such as aphids, ground beetles and grasshoppers.

WILDLIFE WATCH

How can I see farmland wildlife?

● Look for unsprayed strips in crop fields, marked by colourful plants such as cornflower and poppy. These support many insects.

● Don't stray off footpaths without the farmer's permission and make sure you know and obey the Country Code.

◄ The small white, one of the most widespread of all butterflies, survives well on modern farmland where no chemical sprays have been used.

◄ Golden plovers usually nest on open moorland, but they often retreat to farmland in the winter when the weather in the uplands becomes too severe.

Roadside verges

Thousands of miles of grassy verges line Britain's road network. In summer, they are alive with butterflies and bees, lured by the bright colours of wild flowers. In turn, young birds and small mammals provide rich pickings for foxes and owls.

A roadside is not the most obvious place to look for wildlife, but it takes only a short journey in summer to appreciate the wonderful variety of wild species that flourish in this grassy environment. In some places the riot of summer flowers is so spectacular that it slows the traffic, and in many areas these roadside refuges are some of the richest wildlife habitats in the locality.

At one time roads and tracks were restricted to higher ground or natural ridges in the landscape, where the ground was naturally dry and hard. However, with advances in engineering technology that began with the Romans, roads soon began to extend across the countryside, and the huge growth in road transport has ensured that roads are now a dominant feature of the landscape.

Roads themselves are just featureless ribbons of tarmac, but most are bordered by strips of infrequently managed land that are left undeveloped to allow for future expansion. These form havens for wildlife, and the habitats that evolve here reflect the geology, climate, altitude and aspect of the area.

On long journeys it is often possible to keep track of the changing landscape by watching the road verges alone, and to observe a gentle transition from lush, wooded valleys to dry, scrubby heath or windswept moorland without leaving the car.

Wildlife corridors

Often unaffected by the more destructive practices of modern agriculture, roadside verges offer ideal routes for animals, such as foxes, that regularly travel long distances, and slower-moving species that are simply spreading farther afield. Uncut roadsides overgrown with brambles have benefited invertebrates such as Roesel's bush cricket, which has recently expanded its breeding range. Birds, too, visit roads. The buzzard, for example, has been able to return to places where it was once common, perhaps partly through taking advantage of the feeding opportunities offered by roadside casualties.

Plants, too, spread along roadsides, advancing a little farther each season. Many are native species, but others are

▲ **The bee orchid often establishes itself alongside roads. In the absence of competition, these and other orchids may form dense colonies.**

▼ **In the first few years after a road is built, the verges are often bright with flowers that flourish in soil that has been disturbed, such as poppies and corn marigolds.**

▼ **Roesel's bush cricket has spread steadily throughout southern England in recent decades, aided by the network of grassy roadside verges.**

▲ The marbled white butterfly can be seen among roadside vegetation in summer in southern Britain, especially on or near chalk downland.

► If verges are cut late in the season, common spotted orchids are likely to appear. This orchid is providing a perch for mating six-spot burnet moths.

One of the most frequently seen birds of motorway and roadside verges is the kestrel. It hovers silently overhead, scanning the long grass for small rodents, such as voles.

introduced plants that have followed roads inland to establish colonies far from the shores where they first appeared, or from the gardens from which they escaped.

The high levels of salt applied to winter roads has increased the range of predominantly coastal, salt-tolerant plants. These include common scurvygrass, the tiny mauve or white flowers of which often dominate the thin vegetation that adorns the central reservations of motorways.

Roadside reserves

The wide, open grassy verges that border motorways provide perfect environs for many wild flowers. The thin, bare soils left in the aftermath of road building are both free-draining and deficient in nutrients – a combination that is ideal for many wild plants that cannot compete with more vigorous species on fertile soil. As a result they are colonised by a variety of colourful plants. It is not uncommon to see big drifts of flowers such as cowslips and even common spotted orchids alongside slip roads and on roundabouts. Many of these will have sprouted from previously dormant seeds aroused by the disturbance of the ground. Some calcareous (lime-rich) verges form unofficial, but nonetheless important, roadside nature reserves where rare plants such as green hounds-tongue and spiked rampion grow, while sandy soils support other rarities such as lesser calamint and red-tipped cudweed.

Many recently created motorway verges have been sown with wild flower seed mixtures, and the bare soils are rapidly transformed into meadow-like slopes. Arable 'weeds' that were once common on field margins flourish here. Field poppies and rarer plants such as corncockle, corn marigold and cornflower are common in seed mixtures and, in the first two years after planting, the flowers of these annual plants turn the verges into tapestries of vivid colour.

Prickly pioneers

On unseeded patches of disturbed ground, early colonising plants such as teasel, spear thistle, foxglove and ragwort form tall, dense stands of brightly coloured flowers, while dandelions and daisies dominate the short swards nearer the road. The pale hairy leaves of white mullein may also be seen.

Native plants growing on road verges attract many insects that feed on both the flowers and the leaves. Painted

▲ Early summer is peak time for the field vole. These small rodents nest in hedges and grasslands alongside roads, attracting airborne hunters, such as kestrels, buzzards and barn owls.

► Ox-eye daisies are an important source of nectar for butterflies. Massed along a roadside, they are a dazzling sight.

DANGER!

Surrounded by fast-moving traffic and often suffering from air pollution, many roadside verges can be hazardous and unpleasant places to visit. Some are also inaccessible without breaking the law.

lady butterflies are lured to the rich purple flowers of the thistles, while hoverflies and bees swarm over the bright yellow blooms of ragwort. Later in the summer, the seed-rich heads of thistles and teasels attract flocks of small birds, especially goldfinches.

In time, the thin vegetation of newly established road verges becomes lush and thick with the perennial flowers and grasses more commonly associated with hay meadows. These mature verges are now

◄ The tawny owl occurs in woodland and areas with scattered timber, but telegraph poles can serve sometimes as makeshift daytime roosts.

considered to be a major stronghold of the field vole. This species has declined over the past century due to changes in agriculture, which have eliminated many of the old pastures that form its main habitat. The narrow grasslands of the roadside that remain undisturbed by intensive management provide small mammals, such as the field vole, with suitable places to live. The roadsides are not without their dangers, however, as predators, such as kestrels and foxes, often patrol the verges in search of prey.

Early flowers

Solar energy absorbed by the dark tarmac and the heat generated by traffic tend to make the average temperature of roadside verges one or two degrees warmer than that of similar habitats away from the

◄ A ready supply of small mammals, such as rabbits and voles, attracts foxes to the verge. Here one hunts boldly in daylight, unperturbed by traffic.

► The dry, sloping banks of many roadside verges are ideal for rabbits to dig their burrows, where their numbers can reach almost plague proportions.

▼ Where the cutting regime prevents shrubs from becoming established, many verges may come to resemble flower-filled meadows, bright with species such as red campion, bluebells and ramsons (wild garlic).

road. The warmth can make wild flowers bloom several weeks before those in nearby meadows, and many verges are already shimmering with ox-eye daisies and white campion in early May.

Insects also emerge earlier, and butterflies such as meadow browns and ringlets are often on the wing several weeks before their meadow-dwelling counterparts. Gorse and bramble-covered verges ring with the calls of bush crickets in summer, and the 'sewing-machine' song of the great green bush cricket – a species of southern Britain – is so loud that it can easily be heard above the traffic noise, and sometimes even from inside the car.

Hot, dry summers are a perilous time for the animals and plants that live near a road – warm air and drying breezes create the tinderbox conditions that lead to fires. A discarded cigarette thrown from a car window can easily ignite the dry grasses, gorse

▲ Resting on a 'cat's eye', this toad will be lucky to survive. Huge numbers of toads are killed as they cross roads to their breeding ponds each year.

twigs and leaf litter that may lie on the verge, and once started, roadside fires often spread rapidly. Such fires are often devastating to the local wildlife, but in the wake of such disasters the charred ground soon springs back into life. The aptly nicknamed 'fireweed', or rosebay willowherb, is often first to appear, and its pink flowers quickly restore colour to the blackened verge.

Night hunters

Roadsides are excellent places to look for night-time predators, such as owls. The long stretches of fencing and scattered ivy-clad trees that line many roads provide perfect perches for these charismatic birds. A twilight drive may provide close views, for owls are often dazzled by

car headlights, and sit motionless until their sensitive vision adjusts to the light.

The ghostly barn owl is one of the most dramatic sights, as its mainly white plumage shows up well against dark foliage. Little owls are found by some verges, and their small, rotund profiles may be spotted in the lower branches of roadside trees, or sitting on fence posts scanning the verge for beetles and moths.

Owls themselves are often struck by cars – roads can be deadly places for birds and animals. As metalled roads carve the countryside into ever smaller pockets of land, more animals must cross them. Roads often

slice through the territories of wide-roaming or migratory species, creating perilous barriers that isolate them from feeding grounds or breeding sites.

Frogs, toads and newts are particularly vulnerable, because they are often forced to cross busy roads on the way to their breeding ponds. In some areas, the seasonal mass migration of toads across the roads can lead to the death of thousands in a single night. Such carnage can severely affect the long-term prospects of an isolated colony.

Millions of animals die every year on the roads, but some species profit from the casualties. Rooks and crows

The pheasant is among the most common road casualties in rural areas, because it often feeds near a road and heavy, reared birds can be poor fliers.

can often be seen stalking the roadside, searching for carrion and large insects that may have bounced off car windscreens. Foraging hedgehogs also find easy pickings on the roadside, but they, too, often end up on the menu for hungry crows.

Magpies have become adept at scavenging from the carcasses of mammals and birds killed on the roads, while avoiding being struck in the process.

Life in an old apple orchard

A long-established orchard offers safe refuge and a well-stocked larder for birds and mammals. The meadow flowers that dot the uncut grass beneath the trees are irresistible to many insects and the apple blossom attracts pollinating bees.

Buzzing with bees and alive with birdsong, an old apple orchard is a glorious place to be on a sunny day. As the fruit swells on the trees, the apples seem to concentrate all the warmth and golden glow of summer in their sweet, fragrant flesh. When they are harvested at the end of the season, they prolong the memory of summer well into the darker days of autumn.

The Romans probably brought the first eating apple varieties to Britain, supplementing the native, but sour-tasting, crab apple. By the 7th century many orchards were established in the grounds of monasteries, where the art of breeding and grafting was developed. The monks introduced further varieties of apple for cider-making and eating.

During the time of the Normans apple orchards were to be found on many manor estates. By the middle of the 19th century, apple breeding had become a popular pastime, and the number of varieties increased rapidly. It was not unknown for a single orchard to contain over 200 different strains. Altogether more than 6000 varieties of apple have been grown in Britain. While commercial apple growing has always been concentrated in the south, different apple varieties could be found from north of Inverness to the tip of Cornwall. Until recently few farms or large gardens were without a tree or two.

Today's commercial apple growers use a tiny proportion of the thousands of varieties developed in the past. The apples are treated with pesticides to ensure they are free of the smallest blemish, because consumer pressure demands that every fruit is the perfect size, shape and colour. This makes most commercial orchards relatively hostile to wildlife, but luckily some old orchards still survive, along with their traditional varieties of apples and a wealth of wild plants and animals.

Apple trees are traditionally planted in regimented lines to make access easy, but this does not make the orchards any less attractive to wildlife.

APPLE TREE FACT FILE

Many apple trees flourish in grassland, woodlands and parks all over the country, although many more are grown in orchards and gardens. The apples produced by most of these trees are larger and sweeter than native crab apples, and the fruit yields from each tree are much greater.

Tall, straggly growth proliferates if the tree is left unpruned.

● NAMES
Common name: apple
Scientific name: *Malus domestica*

● HABITAT
Cultivated in orchards and gardens, but also grows wild; apple trees do not thrive on poor acid soils or in areas that have high rainfall or lie above about 250m (820ft)

● DISTRIBUTION
Throughout British Isles, but most commercial orchards are in the south

● HEIGHT
Usually 6–10m (20–33ft), depending on variety

● LIFESPAN
40–50 years in the wild, but life of orchard trees prolonged or shortened by cultivation

● BARK
Greyish brown; often splits into small, loose, rectangular scales in older trees

● LEAVES
Oval, rounded at base, serrated margins; densely woolly below

● BRANCHES
Young stems covered with woolly down; lack thorns of crab apple

● FLOWERS
5 petals, either white or pink and white; grow in clusters on soft stalks; appear May–June

● FRUIT
Apple is large, invariably more than 5cm (2in) in diameter, varying in colour and taste

● SEEDS
Numerous small, brown, hard-cased 'pips' in central core

● USES
Fruit eaten raw or cooked, juiced or special varieties made into cider; wood is valuable for decorative objects

The centre of the tree has dense, overlapping branches and twigs.

In winter the outline is rounded and domed.

Most English apple varieties acquire a reddish hue as they ripen.

Leaf margins are serrated.

The leaf is oval and has a short stalk.

Flower buds are deep pink.

Cultivated flowers are pinker than wild varieties.

CRAB APPLE

The small, shrub-like crab apple, *Malus sylvestris*, is regarded as a native British tree because it recolonised Britain after the Ice Age. Its frothy pinkish white blossom may be seen in copses, thickets and hedgerows in April and May. The twigs often bear spines and the purplish brown bark grows rough with age.

Wild crab apples, of which there are about 25 species, are small and bitter, with a woody texture. Nevertheless, some varieties are cultivated for their fruit, which is used to make jelly and wine.

Most crab apples remain green for a considerable length of time and do not ripen until late autumn. Despite their appealing colour, they remain extremely sour.

In some old orchards the meadows that lie beneath the trees have never been deliberately reseeded or sprayed with weedkillers. At some time they may have been used to graze sheep or geese, or as convenient places to keep pigs that eat windfall apples in late summer.

These days much of this land is left ungrazed, sometimes to provide crops of hay, and over the years it has developed a glorious variety of wild meadow flowers. In spring, cowslips and primroses can be found among the short grass. Later on in the season, spikes of common spotted and early purple orchids often appear. As summer advances the ground becomes a tapestry of colour, with plants such as meadow buttercup, ox-eye daisy, yellow rattle, red clover, salad burnet and yarrow flowering together.

A brown hare takes refuge among orchard flowers. Longer legs and long, black-tipped ears distinguish hares from rabbits.

Mistletoe clusters

One feature of many old orchards is the mistletoe that often festoons the trees. Mistletoe is a semi-parasitic plant that can be found growing on several species of host trees, including poplars and limes, but apple is the most common. The decline of mistletoe in many areas has been linked to the trend for grubbing out old apple orchards.

The white berries of mistletoe attract a variety of birds, including the blackcap, blue tit and several thrushes. The bird most associated with it, however, is the mistle thrush. These birds eat the berries of hawthorn, yew and holly as well, but an old apple orchard with mistletoe

The bullfinch eats apple buds mainly when wild seeds are scarce. The birds tend to concentrate their attention on the edges of the orchard.

provides them with their favourite food. Mistletoe berries are very sticky, and birds often wipe their bills on tree branches to clean them. In the process they lodge the seeds in bark crevices, and this enables mistletoe to spread from tree to tree. The seeds may also be passed by the birds in their droppings.

Traditional orchards are havens for all kinds of birds, but one of the most colourful – and notorious – is the bullfinch. For most of the year, these dumpy, stout-billed

birds feed off the buds, flowers, fruit and seeds of native hedgerow and woodland plants. In early spring, however, many bullfinches move into apple orchards, where they flit among the

blossom-laden branches, gorging themselves on the emerging buds.

The bullfinch's heavy bill is so well adapted for prising the buds off the stems that a single bird can devour up to 45 buds in a minute. It is hardly surprising, therefore, that the bullfinch has been considered a pest by apple growers, and attempts were made to destroy it or drive it away. However, it is now known that an apple tree can lose up to half of its buds without a major sustained effect on the crop.

Pollinating bees

Nectar-feeding insects such as bees are vital to the success of the apple harvest, for without them the blossom would not be pollinated and the apples would not develop. The tree relies on the bees to brush against the male anthers of the flowers, pick up the pollen and transfer it to the female styles to fertilise them. For this

▶ **Colourful spires of common spotted orchids often sprout through the grass in old orchards and may form large colonies.**

▼ **Clumps of cowslips brighten orchard meadows in spring. The plant thrives only where the ground has not been dug or treated with fertilisers.**

◄ A treecreeper hunts for insects in the deep fissures and crevices of an old apple tree's bark. The tree also provides the bird with nesting and roosting sites.

◄ Mistletoe thrives in apple orchards and does no harm to the trees. Berries appear late in the season and persist into winter.

▲ The mistle thrush feeds on windfall apples as well as mistletoe berries. The birds are highly territorial and will often drive off other thrushes.

reason, many apple growers encourage beekeepers to site beehives in their orchards. Wild bees of various species live among the trees, as do a variety of other insects such as hoverflies, wasps and butterflies, and these also pollinate the blossom.

Voracious caterpillars

The sheltered conditions of most orchards mean that insect life can be found there all year round. The winter moth gets its name from the fact that the male moths are on the wing during early winter, when many other species are hidden away. One of the most common moths of the British Isles, the winter moth is found on most deciduous trees including fruit trees. Its eggs overwinter on the trees and the caterpillars emerge in spring, just in time to feast on the flush of new leaves. They can cause a lot of damage, and, along with other moths, may be serious pests in commercial orchards, but they are also an important source of protein for the spring broods of birds such as the blue tit. Any caterpillars that survive abseil down to the orchard floor on silken threads and burrow into the soil to pupate. They emerge as adults from October to November. The wingless, spider-like females climb into the trees where they mate with the males and lay their eggs.

Another pest is the red spider mite, a creature so small that a hand lens is required to see it. This mite can damage apple trees by sucking the sap from the undersides of leaves. It thrives in hot summers and is difficult to control. Luckily it has a

Large apple orchards are part of the Worcestershire countryside. A good crop depends on spring blossom remaining undamaged following pollination.

Apple orchards are among the habitats favoured by the cirl bunting. This relative of the yellowhammer has been declining in numbers in Britain for the past 70 years. Requiring sunny, frost-free locations, like those in the Mediterranean, it is on the edge of its range in Britain. It has always been more or less restricted to southern England and now it breeds only in south Devon, mainly between Plymouth and Torquay.

At its peak in the mid-1930s the cirl bunting could be found in various habitats, but its preference was for small fields containing elm trees surrounded by thick hedges. Nowadays, fields tend to be much larger than in the past and elms have been all but eliminated by disease. In addition, the trend towards planting winter wheat has meant the loss of unploughed stubble on which the birds could feed in winter.

An old orchard provides an ideal alternative site, where the birds can live and breed. The surrounding hedgerows offer cover and good nesting sites, and the buntings can feed on grass seeds on the ground below the apple trees. When the chicks hatch, their increasing demand for protein-rich insect food is easily met because the meadow grass is alive with bush crickets, grasshoppers and beetles.

An adult cirl bunting must work hard to feed its hungry young, but the insect life in the grass below the trees provides ample prey.

deadly enemy – the black-kneed capsid bug. Unlike most other capsids, which eat plant material, this aptly named insect is a miniature predator that preys heavily on the red spider mite.

Another friend of orchard keepers is the treecreeper. The large claws of this diminutive bird enable it to cling to the bark of an apple tree as it climbs up the trunk, using its fine, downcurved bill to probe nooks and crannies for weevils, earwigs, moths, woodlice and spiders. These small creatures, some of which damage the apple crop, form most of the treecreeper's diet.

Rich juices
Apples contain a lot of sugar, and this source of energy is invaluable for animals that are building up their reserves before the winter sets in. Late summer windfalls of over-ripe fruit attract butterflies, such as the red admiral, comma and tortoiseshell. They gorge themselves on the sweet, often alcoholic juices of the fruit, and their ensuing lethargy makes them easy to watch.

Wasps are also drawn to the feast of fruit. Although they are considered a nuisance by many people, they help to pollinate the apple trees and prey on insect pests, such as moth caterpillars, which they feed to their larvae during the summer months.

Many birds – especially blackbirds, song thrushes, fieldfares and redwings – pick at the fallen fruit. Fieldfares and redwings welcome the nourishment after their long flight south from northern Europe to their wintering grounds in the British Isles.

As dusk settles over the orchard, the cover of darkness allows other animals to feed on the windfalls. Deer, especially roe and muntjac, may pay

▲ Occasionally, a hedgehog will nibble at windfall apples, but it is probably more interested in eating the invertebrates attracted by the fallen fruits.

▶ Rotting fallen apples are a valuable source of food for butterflies such as this red admiral. The emergence of a second generation in late summer coincides with the apple crop.

▲ Comma butterflies are frequent visitors to orchards in autumn. They are easily recognised by the ragged edges to their wings.

a visit to the orchard. Both of these species move alone or in small groups, and are adept at slipping unnoticed into places near human habitation. Other mammals such as hedgehogs, foxes and badgers also come to feed on the apples, and there are several tales of such animals succumbing to the levels of alcohol found in fermenting windfalls. Bemused wood mice and badgers have certainly been spotted, seemingly intoxicated by the natural cider that brews within the rotting fruit.

Orchard survival

During the last four decades more than two-thirds of Britain's old orchards have disappeared. Supermarkets often obtain their fruit from overseas, and remaining growers have turned to intensive cropping. However, the threat to traditional varieties of apples has been recognised. The environmental organisation Common Ground is promoting a campaign to conserve old orchards and create new ones. The apple orchard's contribution not only to fruit growing, but also to Britain's cultural heritage and wildlife, is being acknowledged.

Apple trees laden with fruit in late summer promise a plentiful harvest, both for growers and wildlife. Windfalls sustain birds, insects and mammals through autumn and into winter.

WILDLIFE WATCH

How can I help orchard wildlife?

● In order to find out more about orchards, the wildlife that lives in them and how to get involved in their protection, contact Common Ground at Gold Hill House, 21 High Street, Shaftesbury, Dorset SP7 8JE (telephone 01747 850820) or visit www.commonground.org.uk Common Ground will also advise on old varieties of apples, where to buy plants, and how to grow them – even just one tree.

● To start a miniature orchard, plant between four to eight trees in a regimented manner, making sure that each one is a minimum of 4.5m (15ft) apart. Prune them to ensure each tree has an open canopy accessible for picking fruit, and plant the ground below as a wild flower meadow, using a mixed selection of seeds. Always leave a proportion of apples on the trees and do not remove windfalls. These provide an essential source of food for a wide variety of animals, particularly during the winter months.

● Use old or bruised apples to feed the birds. Keep the apples in a dry, cool and dark place until there is a cold snap, and then put them out in the garden.

Hazel coppice

The ancient practice of coppicing hazel was developed to provide a regular supply of wooden poles and charcoal. Coppices have provided shelter and food for a variety of woodland plants and animals for centuries.

One of the most highly managed forms of woodland, the hazel coppice is subject to regular human intervention that radically alters the nature of the trees and their environment. Fortunately, this type of management encourages wildlife and has been practised for so long – some 4000 years – that the hazel coppice has become a favoured habitat for many plants and animals.

Coppicing involves cutting the growing tree down to the base, leaving just the roots and a very short section of trunk in place in the ground. In the past, the cut trunks and branches were used for traditional woodland products, such as bean poles and pea sticks for gardeners. Split hazel wands were used for making hurdles and thatching spars, and larger sections of wood were set aside for charcoal burning. Charcoal was once the only fuel capable of producing the heat needed to smelt iron, and was extremely valuable. Coppicing was vital to the national economy.

Hazel has a natural lifespan of around 60 years, after which it will succumb to attacks by fungi or storms and die. However, if it is cut down almost to the roots before this, it sends out new stems, which mature to form new woody trunks, and this considerably extends the life of the tree. When the new trunks are cut, the tree will send up more shoots. The process can be repeated again and again, yielding a crop of hazel poles and brushwood every seven to 12 years, so it is a truly sustainable industry.

Habitat mosaic

Hazel thrives on regular coppicing, producing more new growth and consequently more leaves, catkins and nuts each time it is cut back. The original plant becomes a complex multi-stemmed tree, supporting a huge range of wildlife. The practice of coppicing hazel woodland in small blocks, so that each is at a different stage of its growth cycle, produces a whole variety of surroundings, from newly cleared open spaces to dense growth that is ready to be cut. Crab apple, wild cherry (or gean) and guelder rose are among other plants that grow among the hazel, helping to increase this patchwork of habitats.

Coppiced hazel will survive for far longer than a tree left to grow naturally. Relatively young growth sprouts from a broad base that may be hundreds of years old.

HAZEL FACT FILE

The leaves of this deciduous tree have sawtoothed edges and are attached alternately on each side of the stems. Young trees have trunks that are very straight with shiny bark, while the mature trunks of older trees are more gnarled and twisted.

● NAMES
Common names: hazel, common hazel
Scientific name: *Corylus avellana*

● HABITAT
Mainly fertile lowlands, but widely planted

● DISTRIBUTION
Throughout Britain and Ireland

● HEIGHT
3–6m (10–20ft) when mature

● LIFESPAN
Naturally about 60 years, much longer if coppiced, possibly up to several hundred years

● BARK
Shiny, grey-brown; peels away in thin flakes

● LEAVES
Quite large, 5–12cm (2–4¾in) long, rounded and hairy with coarsely toothed margins and pointed tip; often pale purplish brown when young

● STEMS AND BRANCHES
Straight and tall at first, becoming twisted and gnarled with age; twigs hairy at tips

● FLOWERS
Male flowers are long yellow catkins, female flowers are short, erect, red structures, turning into little cones; male and female flowers occur on the same tree and open at the same time

● FRUITS
Nuts produced in clusters of 4–5; encased in woody shells and sitting in leafy, cup-shaped bracts that are split into jagged 'teeth'

● USES
Nuts harvested for food; coppice wood used for bean poles, broom handles, walking sticks, woven hurdles, thatching spars, charcoal, firewood

In winter, hazel trees have dormant catkins and rounded greenish brown buds. The ends of young twigs are reddish, hairy and rough.

◄ Hazel leaves are rounded with serrated margins and pointed tips. The surface is slightly rough to the touch. Some show signs of being nibbled by caterpillars or may contain the burrows of leaf miners, tiny moth caterpillars. In autumn, the leaves turn yellow before falling.

A hazel tree growing naturally in the open has one or two stems and a rounded crown, but coppiced hazels have several narrower stems sprouting from broad rootstocks known as coppice stools.

◄ Hazel nuts appear in clusters. At first they are green, but ripen to brown just before they drop from the tree.

CATKINS

Catkins, sometimes called 'lamb's tails', begin to form in the summer and are difficult to see among the mature leaves. When the leaves have fallen in the autumn the catkins remain on the twigs, looking rather small and green. For most of the winter they remain dormant, but in early spring they grow and change from green to yellow. The scales on the catkins spread open to reveal the yellow anthers. These produce vast quantities of pollen, which is shaken out by the wind. The catkins open before the leaves so that the pollen can be blown easily from one tree to another. The pollen has to reach the tiny female flowers to fertilise them, and enable their capsules to develop into hazel nuts.

When the pollen has been blown away, the catkins will drop off the tree and break up among the debris on the woodland floor.

◄ Hazel nuts are eaten by grey squirrels while still green. Squirrels often strip trees of nuts before they ripen into viable seeds, so even if buried whole they will not sprout into new hazel trees.

◄ Wild cherry, which often thrives alongside hazel, is usually allowed to grow and fruit naturally.

out of fat buds close to the main twigs. When they are fertilised by the wind-blown pollen they start to develop into the hazel nuts that ripen on the tree during August and September.

The leaves open after the flowers have fallen, usually in May. Several moths, such as the nut tree tussock and the green silver lines, lay their eggs on the leaves, and if their caterpillars escape the attention of birds, they will develop into moths in the summer of the following year.

Soon afterwards, fungi may push up through the soil and leaf litter around the coppice stools – a stool is the base of the tree after cutting. Ancient stools can reach massive proportions and may support colonies of lichens and delicate mosses.

Nut harvest

Hazel nuts are of immense importance to the wildlife of the coppice, especially to one species of mammal – the

▲ In many hazel coppices wood anemones form extensive carpets on the woodland floor in spring.

► Fungi, such as this *Russula*, flourish among hazel trees in the misty weeks of late summer and autumn.

dormouse. Known in the rest of Europe as the hazel dormouse, it relies on a good nut crop to accumulate enough body fat to last it through several months of hibernation. The dormouse is small and light enough to scamper to the end of thin twigs where it finds nuts that heavier birds and squirrels cannot reach.

▼ Richly coloured early purple orchids often bloom among the bluebells in older hazel coppices. Here the hazel has just been cut, allowing light to flood the woodland floor.

Hazel often grows beneath far larger trees, such as ash and oak. A type of woodland called 'coppice with standards' is quite common, with tall oak trees grown for timber soaring above coppiced hazel. This is why coppiced hazel is known as 'underwood'.

Leaves and flowers

The hazel is a familiar small tree of the countryside, found all over the British Isles as far north as Orkney. It was among the first deciduous trees to recolonise the land at the end of the Ice Age, so is one of the most well-established native trees. It grows well on most soils and in most climates, but it cannot grow in deep shade. When grown with oaks, for example, the big timber trees have to be well spaced to allow the hazel to thrive.

In summer hazel is quite easy to identify by its relatively large, round or heart-shaped leaves, with their pointed tips and serrated edges. However, it is more easily recognised in the spring, long before the leaves open, by its dangling yellow catkins. These grow abundantly on mature trees that are exposed to plenty of light. Catkins are male flowers and the clouds of yellow pollen they produce can be seen drifting from them when they are caught by the wind.

The female flowers are less obvious. These are tiny red star-like structures that grow

► Crab apple trees often fruit well in newly coppiced areas because of the increased light. The apples, which normally remain green until they drop, can sometimes be colourful and look inviting, but they are always very sour.

As summer turns to autumn the leaves of guelder rose turn red, and the branches are soon festooned with luscious-looking berries that are rapidly eaten by birds.

BLOOMING IN THE LIGHT

Mature stands of hazel cast a heavy shade on the woodland floor, so plants that require plenty of light do not thrive in hazel woodland that is not coppiced. A few mosses, ferns and fungi may be found, but most of the ground layer consists of fallen leaves. In the first year after coppicing, however, so much light floods in that the ground flora is rejuvenated, and what was once a carpet of leaf litter becomes green with the leaves of plants that have lain dormant for many years. They include wood anemones, or windflowers, which are stimulated to produce their delicate nodding white flower heads when warmed by the sun. These plants can exist in a vegetative state for years without flowering, but as the light increases they burst into bloom. It is thought that they rarely set seed in Britain, relying on their fleshy rhizomes (underground stems) to spread through the woodland.

The delicate wood sorrel, with its down-turned, clover-like leaves and pink-veined white flowers, is rarely found outside woodlands, because it is unable to tolerate the heat and brightness of too much direct sunlight. It too spreads via rhizomes when living in shady conditions, but when the hazel is coppiced the wood sorrel takes advantage of the light and increased number of pollinating insects to produce more flowers and set seeds.

Many other species of wild flowers exploit the sudden change in conditions to flower prolifically for the first few years after the trees are coppiced. Foxgloves produce leaf rosettes in their first year and then, because they are biennials, develop their tall flower spikes in the second year after coppicing. Wild daffodils, greater stitchwort, yellow pimpernel, primroses and bugle enliven the woodland floor for a few seasons until the shady canopy closes in once more. Much depends on soil types and climate – on some heavy clay soils primroses proliferate, but where the soil is lighter, as on chalkland, the ground is covered with the fresh green of dog's mercury.

▼ Wild daffodils that may not have flowered for several years suddenly produce flowers after the trees have been cut.

▲ Spikes of bugle adorn the woodland floor where trees have been coppiced in the past three years.

▲ The trailing yellow pimpernel flourishes in recently cleared areas of hazel woodland, and along the open, sunlit margins and rides.

Some animals store hazel nuts as a winter food supply, and compete with each other to collect and hoard them when they are ripe. The yellow-necked mouse, for example, makes large caches of hazel nuts in hollow trees or bird nestboxes.

Another hoarder is the grey squirrel, which gathers hazel nuts in large numbers, even before they are ripe, and buries them in the woodland floor. The hazel's fertility is now compromised in much of Britain by the activities of the grey squirrel.

Juicy shoots

Left to themselves, old trees would die and decay, but when the top growth is harvested the stump sends out vigorous new stems that are highly palatable to deer. If shoots are nibbled, the tree may simply produce more, rather in the way that pruned roses sprout when cut back. However, if the browsing is too intensive, the hazel may not recover, and it could die after one or two years. So if too many deer are attracted to the hazel, the stools are given protection. Brushwood is often piled over them to disguise their presence, or the area that has been coppiced may be fenced off to keep the deer out until the shoots are tall enough to be out of reach.

▼ **Hazel nuts, in both their developing and mature stages, are vital to the survival of the common or hazel dormouse. The energy that the nuts contain enables the dormouse to build up the reserves of fat it needs to see it through the winter.**

BREEDING BUTTERFLIES

Coppicing provides the warmth, light and abundant wild flowers that give some butterflies exactly what they need to breed. They include the small pearl-bordered fritillary, once known as the 'woodman's follower' as it was likely to turn up in hazel woods a year or so after they had been coppiced. A fresh growth of common dog violets or marsh violets – the foodplants of the caterpillars – and an increase in nectar-producing plants such as bugle and bramble (which provide nectar for the adults) help to ensure the survival of these scarce butterflies. They do not usually scatter very far but as long as a new area is coppiced each year and is within range of the butterflies, they are able to move around the woodland from one clearing to another. The much larger silver-washed fritillary also takes advantage of these new clearings, and other more common species – including the speckled wood and green-veined white butterflies – will have a few good breeding years until the canopy closes in again.

◄ **One of the biggest British butterflies, the silver-washed fritillary, often breeds in coppices.**

▲ **A mating pair of brimstones rests on a bluebell plant. The female is paler and greener than the yellower male.**

In areas with a high deer population, their browsing may prevent the growth of all but the hardiest and most unpalatable plants. Where there are no deer at all the woodland floor may be taken over by a luxuriant growth of plants, but this may crowd out delicate species that are unable to compete with faster-growing plants. Limited grazing pressure from deer seems to achieve the right balance, giving delicate species the space they need to grow.

Wild flowers

One of the glories of the hazel coppice is the mass of bluebells that often covers the ground with colour in spring and early summer. Although a very familiar plant in Britain, the bluebell is far less common in the rest of Europe, where the climate is generally drier. In hazel coppices bluebells often monopolise the woodland floor, and the blue haze of flowers is only occasionally punctuated by other species, such as the early purple orchid, red campion, Solomon's-seal and herb-Paris. Bluebells spread very slowly, either by seed or by dividing bulbs, and the sight of tens of thousands of bluebells covering the forest floor usually indicates that the woodland is very ancient.

Birds and coppicing

Newly coppiced areas are too open for true woodland birds to benefit from them, but once the hazel has started to regenerate, the insect life increases rapidly and food becomes available for warblers, thrushes, tits and other insectivorous birds. After two to three years a dense scrub of hazel, bramble and ferns may have built up, which allows small birds such as the chiffchaff and willow warbler to find places to nest. After a few more years,

▲ **The yellow-necked mouse thrives in hazel coppices and other deciduous woodland. It occurs in southern and south-eastern England.**

▲ Once coppiced woodland has acquired a layer of brambles and other scrub, a garden warbler may breed there. The caterpillars that eat the hazel foliage provide plenty of food.

▲ Tangled vegetation and fallen leaves provide cover for a chiffchaff to nest in the undergrowth. This tiny warbler is one of the first migrants to return each year.

▲ Roe deer are common among coppiced hazel. The deer look for patches of thick cover where they can lie up during the day, venturing out to feed at dawn or dusk.

as the hazel matures, the ground flora diminishes and the insect population is reduced, but another species then begins to benefit. Impenetrable hazel thickets are ideal for the nightingale, and for a few years, before the coppice becomes derelict or is cut once more, the thickets may ring to this summer visitor's famously melodious song. The nightingale is heard at its best in the still of the night, when other species are quiet, but in spring it can also be heard during the day, its

fluty, chuckling, croaking and trilling notes clearly audible above the songs of willow warblers and blackcaps.

When the hazel is fully mature it once more becomes the haunt of woodland birds, such as the robin and wren, and is a rather quiet place until the hazels are cut and the cycle begins again.

Derelict coppices

Unfortunately, many hazel woods are no longer coppiced on a regular basis, and are turning into ordinary woodland. The loss of the varied habitats associated with coppicing may be one reason for the decline in woodland bird numbers. As the woodlands become shadier, carpets of spring flowers, such as the bluebell, also become thinner, and may disappear altogether in some places.

However, the seeds and roots often remain viable for many years, and if the trees are coppiced again, the flowers may spring up to restore the wood to its former glory.

▲ In spring and summer, the song of the nightingale can be heard emanating from mature hazel coppices. It rarely sings from an open perch like this, and is usually extremely difficult to see.

TEN-YEAR CYCLE

● **Year 0:** Amid the dense growth of old, gnarled hazel trunks, a few ferns and mosses grow and a good crop of fungi may appear in the autumn. Robins, wrens and dunnocks nest in the trees. The nut crop is at a low level.

● **Year 1:** During the winter all old trunks are removed. Sunlight reaches the woodland floor and leaf rosettes of foxgloves, orchids and primroses appear. Violets and wood anemones flower and are visited by insects. Hazel shoots start to grow in spring and deer move in to eat them. Thrushes and blackbirds feed on the woodland floor, but they do not nest among the hazel.

● **Year 2:** Foxgloves, bluebells, daffodils and other spring flowers are at their best. Hazel shoots grow longer and deer continue to browse on them. Bramble scrub develops. Insect life increases and fritillary butterflies are more common – speckled wood, brimstone and green-veined white butterflies flit among the flowers. Warblers, robins and wrens visit to feed on insects.

● **Years 3–5:** The hazel and bramble form thickets in which deer hide. By now, the tallest shoots are out of their reach. Bird life increases and warblers nest in scrub patches. Ground flora is still abundant, but shade increases in some areas and some of the plants flower less freely.

● **Years 6–9:** The hazel matures and produces catkins followed by its first full crop of nuts. Dormice and other small mammals move in to feed and nest. Grey squirrels invade to exploit the nut crop. Nightingales may colonise in the south, but warblers become scarcer. Ground flora starts to thin out as the hazel coppice thickens and shades the woodland floor. Deer pass through or shelter, but can find little food.

● **Year 10+:** The mature hazel reaches its full height, and its growth rate slows down. The nut crop reaches its peak and small mammals flourish, but the gound flora and butterfly populations are greatly reduced. Hazel poles are ready for harvesting once more.

The Chilterns

Celebrated for their natural beauty, the extensive beechwoods and chalk grasslands of the Chilterns are famous for rare plants and animals, including some flowers that are found nowhere else in Britain.

Stretching from the Thames at Goring in the south to Hitchin and Stevenage in the north, the Chilterns are a ridge of chalk hills like the North and South Downs. Their chalk downland character is most marked on the steep scarp slopes that face the Vale of Aylesbury to the north-west. Elsewhere the terrain is a more intimate network of wooded ridges and valleys, and over much of the region the chalk is hidden beneath a layer of the aptly named 'clay with flints'. Despite this, most of the rain that falls on the Chilterns

The well-drained, chalky soils of the Chiltern ridges support a wide variety of plants. The number of species is increased where sheep and rabbits nibble the turf, since this stops any one species of plant becoming dominant.

drains straight into the porous chalk below, and few permanent streams flow through the countryside. It is a landscape of secret valleys and hidden corners, with quiet woodland and, in summer, wildly unkempt meadows full of flowers and butterflies.

Wild woods

The Chilterns are among the most heavily wooded parts of England, comparable in extent to the Weald, the New Forest and the Wye Valley. Many of the woods are ancient in origin, with a complex history of management that has fostered a wide variety of plant and animal life.

Beech is the dominant tree in many of the woodlands, having been deliberately planted, or encouraged, in order to provide timber for

the furniture industry that once thrived around High Wycombe. The beeches cast a heavy shade in summer that inhibits the growth of shrubs and woodland flowers. As a result, relatively few insects such as butterflies are to be seen near ground level in the beechwoods. Oak and ash are also common, however, forming mixed woodlands that support a much greater variety of wildlife. Their sunny rides and open clearings are the haunts of butterflies such as speckled wood, orange-tip and green-veined white.

The mixed woodland also supports a greater variety of birdlife than the beechwoods do. Chaffinches, nuthatches, great spotted and green woodpeckers, and various species of tit are plentiful, but other less familiar species

may also be seen. In summer, migrants such as the spotted flycatcher, blackcap and wood warbler breed in many places. Woodcock, which nest among the fallen leaves, can sometimes be seen and heard at dusk performing their special display flights.

Chalk grassland

Patches of flower-rich chalk grassland are found on the escarpments and along the sides of many of the dry valleys, where the chalk juts out from the clay with flints. Many of the best sites are now nature reserves, including Ivinghoe Beacon, Dancersend and the Crong Meadow near Berkhamsted, and Coombe Hill near Princes Risborough.

Almost all the common chalkland plants can be found, such as wild thyme, eyebright, salad burnet, trefoils, clovers and vetches, plus some other species, such as grassland orchids and gentians, that are uncommon or even absent elsewhere in the south of England.

The chalk grassland of the Chilterns is renowned for the variety of butterflies that it supports. Of particular interest are members of the blue family, including the chalkhill blue, common blue and brown argus. More widespread species include the small heath and marbled white. Dingy and grizzled skippers also make an appearance. The silver-spotted skipper – a late summer butterfly – is a speciality of a few grassland sites, and is best looked for in the early morning when its daily cycle of activity is beginning. Two other notable species are the Duke of Burgundy and the dark green fritillary.

Breeding songbirds that frequent the grassland of the region include the meadow pipit, skylark and yellowhammer. The rare and declining corn bunting also nests here. Hovering kestrels and soaring buzzards are a common sight, and during the winter months short-eared owls occasionally patrol the grassy slopes in search of small mammals and birds. The most spectacular of the Chilterns' birds of prey, however, is the red kite, reintroduced to the region and now thriving in good numbers.

Sparkling streams

Many of the chalk streams flowing off the Chilterns are spring-fed, and their upper sections run dry during the summer. This seasonality has given rise to the name 'winterbournes'. In early summer, however, they may still be flowing, and at this time many are covered with white drifts of flowering water-crowfoot, sheltering abundant insect life. Meanwhile, the margins are lined with watercress, yellow iris and several species of marsh orchid.

The chalk streams and their muddy margins are important habitats for fish such as bullheads (also known as 'miller's thumbs') and sticklebacks, as well as brown trout, dace and grayling. The lime-rich water is ideal for the native white-clawed crayfish, which needs calcium to build its shell.

INTRODUCED SPECIES

The Chiltern woodlands are the main home of the fat (or edible) dormouse in Britain. A native of central Europe, this rotund, bushy-tailed rodent owes its presence in the region to introductions made to Tring Park in about 1902. The animals subsequently escaped and established a viable wild population, but since then the species has not spread much.

The fat dormouse looks more like a small grey squirrel than the native common dormouse, but it shares with the latter the habit of hibernating during the winter months. It seems to favour mixed woodland, including mature mixed plantations, but it will sometimes venture into suburban gardens and outbuildings. It may even take up residence in the lofts of houses, but its noisy activities make it an unwelcome guest.

A more recent addition to Chiltern wildlife is the red kite, a magnificent bird of prey that has been reintroduced to the region by English Nature in conjunction with the RSPB. Today, a thriving population is centred around the Stokenchurch area, to the west of High Wycombe, and the birds are easy to see. They can be identified by their long wings with large white patches on their undersides, acrobatic flight, distinctive forked tails and mainly russet plumage. They are especially conspicuous when soaring above their hill and woodland territory on dry, sunny days in spring.

► **Although usually seen in flight, red kites can also be found perched in trees, where they adopt an upright posture with the tail hanging down.**

◄ **Tree holes provide ideal daytime retreats for the fat dormouse. Unlike the red kite, it is an elusive, nocturnal species that is very rarely seen.**

CHILTERN FLOWERS

Spring comes early to the Chilterns with twiggy bushes of mezereon bursting into pink flower in February. The less showy green hellebore and spurge-laurel can also be found in bloom, their flowers attracting early pollinators such as bumblebees in mild weather.

As temperatures rise, typical woodland plants, including bluebell, wood anemone and greater stitchwort, appear wherever light penetrates the canopy. Pride of place, however, must go to coralroot bittercress, an attractive relative of

lady's-smock. The beechwoods of the Chilterns are one of its British strongholds.

In summer, when mature beech trees create dense shade, careful searching among the carpet of golden leaves may reveal yellow bird's-nest – a curious plant that feeds entirely off dead matter, in the same way as a fungus.

A plant with a similar way of life is the extremely rare ghost orchid. It owes its name to the fact that it is entirely lacking in green chlorophyll, and since it does not need leaves it sprouts only when it is ready to flower. Until recently, it grew just in the Chilterns but a lack of recent sightings suggests that it may be extinct. Even if the ghost orchid does appear it does not last for long, for it is soon eaten by slugs. Other woodland orchids include the narrow-lipped helleborine, red helleborine and the very rare, protected military orchid.

◄ In Britain the Chiltern gentian is virtually restricted to the Chiltern region, although it is common in France.

◄ The ghost orchid grows in deep shade among beech leaves. It is extremely rare, and has not been seen for many years.

▼ Another rarity, the military orchid grows in a couple of woodland sites in the Chilterns.

The short, springy turf of the grasslands is of special interest for its wide range of chalkland plants. A succession of familiar species appears throughout the season, including cowslip, field scabious, milkwort, mignonette, salad burnet, yellow rattle, dropwort, kidney vetch and horseshoe vetch. Pasqueflower, one of the most stunning chalk-loving plants, blooms in spring on short turf, and in summer wild candytuft, another Chiltern speciality, can be found.

The grasslands are the home of a variety of colourful orchids, including the common spotted,

▲ Wild candytuft thrives on disturbed chalky soil, and can often be found growing on the lime-rich spoil dug out by rabbits from their burrows.

fragrant, pyramidal, bee and musk orchids. Three rare gentians thrive on a few sites. The diminutive early gentian grows in extremely short turf in spring, and the fringed and Chiltern gentians appear in late summer and autumn, which is long after most other plants have finished flowering. The fringed gentian is a comparative newcomer, and is found nowhere else in Britain. Other members of the gentian family that grow on the Chilterns' grasslands include felwort – also known as autumn gentian – yellow-wort and common centaury.

▼ The lemon slug is one of the less conspicuous Chiltern rarities, most likely to be seen feeding on fungi in autumn.

◄ Chiltern beechwoods have a scenic beauty throughout the year, but they are at their most spectacular in autumn when the beech leaves turn glorious shades of gold and russet.

Places to visit in the Chilterns

Given the comparatively small area encompassed by the Chilterns, and their accessibility from cities and major towns, they are remarkably rich in flourishing wildlife habitats. Few places can offer such a rewarding combination of natural beauty and fascinating plants and animals, including many national rarities.

1 Bradenham Woods
Near Walter's Ash, north of High Wycombe, Bradenham Woods have mature oak and beech trees. Visit in the spring for birds and flowers, or in autumn to find an abundance of fungi.

2 Aston Woods
Located at Chinnor, these ancient and extensive beechwoods have displays of woodland flowers – including the violet helleborine – in spring and summer, as well as fungi in autumn.

3 Chesham Bois Woods
Best known for their bluebells and mature beech trees, Chesham Bois Woods are situated between Amersham and Chesham.

4 Aston Rowant National Nature Reserve
Near Thame and Stokenchurch, this nature reserve has superb chalk grassland with numerous orchids and thriving butterfly populations.

5 Chinnor Hill
The chalk downland and scrub of Chinnor Hill, near Princes Risborough, supports Chiltern gentians.

6 The Warburg Reserve
Located near Henley on Thames, the Warburg Reserve combines woodland, scrub and grassland habitats. It is excellent for woodland butterflies and chalkland plants, and many breeding amphibians frequent its ponds.

7 Watlington Hill
This chalk grassland site is one of the best places to watch for red kites soaring over the hills.

Miles 0   5   10
Km 0   5   10   15

In the past many of the chalk streams were exploited for such purposes as milling and watercress farming, and in places the remains of old mills and abandoned watercress beds can still be found.

Some of the streams in the Chilterns have gained notoriety in recent summers, when drought conditions and over-extraction of water have caused more extensive stretches than usual to dry up completely. The results can make stark viewing as the watercourses are transformed into barren-looking cracked mud dotted with dead fish.

Today, much of the Chiltern landscape is covered by arable farmland. Owing to modern intensive farming methods, wildlife interest is mainly confined to its boundaries but there are still small pockets of land that, because of thin, crumbly soils, are farmed less intensively. These support many now rare plants, such as pheasant's-eye and ground-pine. It seems quite appropriate that they should survive in a region that, despite its proximity to London and several busy towns, has the atmosphere of a truly rural landscape.

WILDLIFE WATCH

When should I visit the Chilterns?

● The chalk grassland sites are best visited in July and August. Most flowers and butterflies are at their best at this time of year, although some of the plants wither by late summer in dry seasons. To see felwort, Chiltern gentian and fringed gentian, come back in September or even October.

● In spring, coralroot bittercress, herb-Paris, green hellebore and mezereon can be seen in the woodlands. In summer, look for orchids such as bird's-nest orchid and violet helleborine. These grow in mature, undisturbed beechwoods in deep shade. The rare and elusive ghost orchid may grow here, too.

● Red kites are often seen in the Stokenchurch area and areas to the south and west at any time of year. Sunny days are best, when the birds can soar on rising thermals. They are generally most active between 10am and 3pm.

Animals and plants in focus

Grassland watch

- The common shrew
- The field vole
- The skylark
- The lapwing
- Burnet moths
- Recognising downland butterflies
- The glow-worm
- Poppies
- Clovers

The common shrew

Long, delicate whiskers and a keen sense of smell help the common shrew to find its way around its territory. Shrill squeaks may be heard when one of these tiny mammals inadvertently strays into another's domain.

Even though it is one of Britain's most abundant mammals, the common shrew is rarely seen because it spends most of its time underground. It forages for insects and earthworms in the soil or leaf litter, scurrying along tiny tunnels and runways that it digs for itself or that have been made by other small mammals.

The common shrew's most readily identifiable feature is its long and pointed snout. This seems to be in constant motion, seeking out the scent of potential prey under stones and in between leaves and grasses. Shrews have small ears and poor eyesight and in the dark depths of their tunnels they rely heavily on their sense of smell.

Identifying shrews

While it is easy to recognise a shrew, it is harder to decide which of the three British mainland species it is – water, pygmy or common. Water shrews can be identified by the colour of their fur, which is black above and silvery white below. Separating pygmy shrews from common shrews is more difficult, although the pygmy shrew is smaller. In pygmy shrews, the tail is at least three-quarters as long as the head and body, while the tails of common shrews are always less than half the length of the head and body. In all shrews the sexes look similar, especially the juveniles, and a magnifying glass is necessary to tell males from females.

The common shrew spends much of its time underground hunting for all types of insects and grubs. It locates its prey by scent.

ABSENT FROM IRELAND

At the end of the last Ice Age, about 10–15,000 years ago, melting ice caused the sea-level to rise. This flooded low-lying land and so the land-bridge that linked Ireland and Britain disappeared under water. Before this happened, various species successfully spread into Ireland but the common shrew was not among them. It appears that this hyperactive animal was unable to find enough to eat in the waterlogged, boggy conditions of the land-bridge, so it was forced to remain on the mainland.

COMMON SHREW FACT FILE

Found almost everywhere in Britain, apart from Ireland and some islands, the common shrew is a prolific breeder. Juveniles survive the winter without hibernation, living on a diet of earthworms and other soil-borne invertebrates.

● NAMES
Common name: common shrew
Scientific name: *Sorex araneus*

● HABITAT
Woodland, farmland and hedgerow

● DISTRIBUTION
Throughout mainland Britain and on many offshore islands, but absent from Ireland, the Scilly Isles and the Channel Islands; tends to be less abundant at high altitudes

● STATUS
Nearly 42 million individuals; population peaks in summer

● SIZE
Head and body 50–80mm (2–3¼in), tail length 30–50mm (1¼–2in), weight 5–12g (¼–½oz)

● KEY FEATURES
Very small, brown all over with lighter brown flanks and pale belly; long, pointed nose, small ears, tiny eyes

● HABITS
Active day and night in long grass, under shrubs and below ground; frequent short periods of rest

● VOICE
Usually twitters; utters loud, piercing squeaks and screams when angry or alarmed

● FOOD
Largely invertebrates, especially earthworms, slugs, snails, insect larvae and beetles; occasionally vertebrates

● BREEDING
Usual litter 6 or 7, but sometimes as many as 10; 2 litters per season (rarely 3 or 4), born April–September

● NEST
A ball of interwoven dried grass and small leaves, constructed under logs, grass tussocks or in burrows of other species

● YOUNG
Paler brown than adult with less sharp demarcation between upper and undersides; tail covered with short bristly hair

● SIGNS
Visual signs are too small to notice, but loud squeaks of aggression or fear are frequently heard

Baby common shrews are born in a grassy nest, which is often built underground. They take a week or so to begin to grow fur and their eyes open after two weeks.

Distribution map key

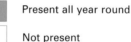
Present all year round

Not present

Dark fur on the back contrasts with the pale belly, especially in winter.

The common shrew's eyes are small and its eyesight weak.

A hairy tail is a sign of youth – the hairs wear off with time so that adults' tails are hairless.

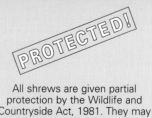

PROTECTED!

All shrews are given partial protection by the Wildlife and Countryside Act, 1981. They may not be deliberately trapped or killed without a special licence.

◀ Like all shrews, the common shrew has a long, narrow and highly mobile snout furnished with long whiskers. It constantly sniffs its surroundings and uses its whiskers to feel its way.

▼ Shrews can climb quite well and often scramble into bushes and shrubs where they may occasionally be found sheltering briefly in bird nestboxes.

The bodies of common shrews are often found lying on footpaths, displaying no obvious cause of death. This has been interpreted as 'dying of shock' and the shrew has a reputation for being highly strung and sensitive. It is a widespread belief that a thunderstorm will cause them to die of fright. In fact, shrews are robust creatures and certainly no more likely to die of fright than any other creature, including humans. The reason so many are found in this way is that predators find shrews' powerful scent glands distasteful. A fox, for example, may successfully pursue and catch a shrew, but will then discard it because it tastes so unpleasant. Likewise, a cat may also catch and kill a shrew but will rarely eat it.

Shrews' scent glands are oval-shaped structures, positioned on their flanks, about midway between the fore and hind limbs. The glands produce a greasy, sweaty substance, which the shrew smears on to any twigs or stones it brushes against. The substance gives the animals a distinctive odour, even to a human's relatively poorly developed sense of smell. The unpleasant scent is usually enough to put off predators such as weasels and stoats, as well as foxes and many other carnivores, but birds of prey generally have a bad sense of smell and are not

Fighting off outsiders

Shrews share runways in the undergrowth with voles and other rodents. However, a chance encounter with another shrew from outside their own family quickly turns into a fierce battle.

A common shrew gives another shrew that has intruded on to its territory little chance to retreat before attacking.

deterred. Shrews often form up to a third or more of the prey (by numbers) eaten by barn owls, for example.

Ferocious fighters

Shrews are solitary animals and very belligerent towards each other. Indeed, a common sign of the presence of shrews is their loud and piercing squeaks when they meet in the undergrowth and engage in noisy confrontations. Often the two opponents will rear up on their hind legs and scratch at each other, squeaking violently all the time, while bearing their red-tipped teeth. Sometimes they grapple, rolling over and over together. When one shrew runs away, the other may pursue it, aiming bites at the retreating shrew's rump and tail. Such open aggression stems from the fact that shrews are not sociable creatures. Each one has its own home territory and keeps itself to itself.

An individual shrew's territory comprises around 500 square metres (5400 square feet), perhaps a little less in winter, which it fiercely defends against

FEEDING HABITS

Throughout its short life, a common shrew is rarely still for more than a few minutes at a time. Its brief periods of rest – at two or three-hour intervals – are usually spent in the safety of the nest, but sometimes a secure place under cover will suffice. Active periods are spent searching for food, and shrews rarely have far to look as the soil teems with worms, woodlice, beetles, caterpillars and a host of other tiny creatures that make up the shrew's diet.

The millions of shrews in Britain eat so many invertebrates that they should be considered true friends of the gardener as well as the farmer. Consumption of caterpillars, baby slugs and beetle larvae alone is enormous, providing a great service to the crops and flowers on which these creatures normally inflict so much damage. Most prey items

Shrews will occasionally take carrion to supplement their diet. This one has found a dead greenfinch. Dead bodies also attract beetles and flies, providing still more welcome food items for a hungry shrew.

are 5–10mm (¼–⅜in) long, but sometimes a large earthworm may be tackled, the head attacked first to paralyse it. Shrews are not particularly fussy, so everything is taken as it comes – only plant material and some bad-tasting millipedes are generally avoided. Large items such as grasshoppers may have their legs bitten off first.

One of the shrew's most curious feeding habits is called 'refection'. This is when the animal sits up, protrudes its rectum and proceeds to lick it clean. The purpose of this odd behaviour may be to obtain additional nutrients from partially digested food and from the bacteria that live in the gut.

Shrews must eat about 90 per cent of their own body weight every day, so

they are always alert for any potential prey. Their noses, whiskers and ears are incredibly sensitive and in such a miniature world, the smallest insect seems noisy as it blunders around. The shrew's sharp senses can locate food that is more than 10cm (4in) deep in the soil. Once prey is detected, the shrew promptly thrusts its snout into every minute nook and crevice that might conceal edible creatures.

Much of the shrew's food consists of earthworms, which are full of water and dirt, so they weigh a lot but contain little nutritional value. Shrews must eat large quantities of them in order to produce the energy they need. Their diet is supplemented with chitin, the more nutritious but indigestible outer covering of insects.

An earthworm is a favourite item in the common shrew's diet. It may struggle to eat a large worm such as this, but will not resist the challenge because the prize is enough food to last for several hours.

The battle is fast and furious, accompanied by much squeaking and lashing of tails.

Eventually one combatant, usually the intruder, extricates itself from the fight and runs off, leaving the victor, still baring its sharp teeth and squeaking, in sole control of its domain.

► Juvenile shrews have a short dark summer coat which fades into brown on the belly. There is less of a sharp demarcation line between the fur of the upper and lower body than in adults.

other shrews. It will remain on its own patch throughout its short life. The marks left on stones, twigs and burrows by its strong scent glands probably serve as warning signs to keep intruders away.

In spring, though, usually in March, the shrew relaxes its territorial instincts a little so that breeding can take place. Males venture into the territories of nearby females, while females become more tolerant of visitors but only for a short time. There is no real courtship and mating is not a prolonged affair. The male and female shrew separate immediately after copulating and probably never meet again. The female will aggressively rebuff any more males that approach her until she is ready to mate again.

To get a better grip during mating, the male often grasps the female by the scruff of the neck with his teeth. This sometimes damages her hair follicles so that although new fur grows, the replacement hairs lack any colour and are a distinguishing pure white. The tuft

► At birth, baby shrews are tiny, hairless and feeble. However, their prodigious appetites mean that they will increase their body weight by 10 times in the first two weeks of life.

Fast food

The shrew lives at a hectic pace, burning a huge amount of energy, which it replenishes by eating plenty of worms and insects. It takes only short periods of rest because if a mere three hours should pass between meals, it would die of starvation.

Emerging cautiously after a short rest, the ever-hungry shrew uses its sensitive nose and whiskers to pick up the scent or vibrations of the smallest prey. A nearby woodlouse stands no chance of passing undetected.

of white hair, or the scars, that many adult females display on the back of the neck are evidence of previous matings.

Caravan of shrews

Female common shrews can sometimes give birth to as many as 10 young, but litters of six or seven are more common. The babies are born pink, blind and without fur, but even at this stage they have the distinctively long shrew's snout. At 16 days old their eyes open, and at three weeks of age they are beginning to feed themselves. At this time, the young may leave the nest in a 'caravan'. The mother leads her family, each youngster hanging on by its teeth to the rump of the one in front. In another week, the young leave for good, going off to find their own territories.

Only about a quarter of young shrews survive to breed. Most die when very young. Despite this, in the summer 50 or more common shrews may inhabit a hectare (2½ acres) of woodland or thick grassland. Later in the year, however, the death of the adult generation,

◀ Damp mossy places attract the common shrew because plenty of insects and other prey are always available. Snails may be eaten occasionally but are generally safe inside their shells.

coupled with high juvenile mortality, reduces numbers by more than half, with sometimes as few as five per hectare (2½ acres) left.

Rapidly growing young

At birth, the babies weigh just half a gram each. The whole litter weighs less than the mother. However, within two weeks of birth each baby will have grown to a weight of about 7g (¼oz), the mother feeding the family of new shrews using her own nutritious milk. This is a tremendous effort on her part, and she has to consume more than her own weight of food every day in order to absorb the necessary nutrients for the energy needed.

Breeding is a herculean task for a female shrew, yet once her young are independent, she may start all over again and have another litter. In one summer, a female may have up to four litters, although one or two is more usual. Any later ones tend to comprise fewer young. By the end of the season, about September, the females are exhausted and most die soon afterwards. Shortly after this, most males reach the end of their natural lifespan and they, too, die. Only a tiny percentage of animals live to be one year old and none exceed 23 months in the wild. The species survives over winter thanks to the juveniles born the previous summer.

Changing fur patterns

When they become independent, juvenile shrews are a pale brown all over. Come the autumn, they begin to moult their summer coat of short hairs which is replaced by a new longer and darker coat of sleek fur for the winter. The moult begins on the rump and progresses towards the head. In October, when the shrews are about halfway through this process, they look as though they are wearing a pair of dark baggy trousers, with the thick new fur only on their hind quarters. By November, the change of coat is complete and the animal is now dark chocolate brown, almost black, with a distinct contrast between the paler fur

▲ A shrew sniffs the air for prey, but in doing so risks some danger to itself. Shrews rarely come out into the open because they are easily snatched by predatory birds, especially owls.

of the belly and darker back. In the spring the reverse takes place, this time starting on the head and moving towards the rear. The long dark fur of winter is shed and replaced by a shorter summer coat, which is also dark in colour. The tail hairs are not moulted and regrown, so the tail gets steadily more hairless as the animal gets older and hairs are worn off it. This helps to distinguish adults from juveniles, which have a comparatively hairy tail like that of the pygmy shrew. Also, the tails of older shrews often bear the scars of aggressive encounters with other shrews.

Another puzzling development occurs in the autumn. Instead of fattening up for the winter as most mammals do, shrews shrink by a quarter. Even their skull and bones get smaller, then regain full size the following year. Exactly how they manage this feat is uncertain and its biological significance is obscure. However, the weight loss obviously does them no harm, since enough shrews always manage to survive to repopulate the countryside in the spring.

The field vole

Leaving the safety of its burrow to feed is risky for the field vole. Scampering through its well-worn runways through the long grass, it is concealed from predatory birds but is still vulnerable to attack from foxes and badgers.

This small mammal plays a crucial part in the natural foodchain. Few of Britain's predators could maintain their present populations without the field vole. Wildcats, pine martens and weasels all depend heavily on this species for food, as do many predatory birds. For example, in most places, at least half of all the animals caught by barn owls are field voles. They are also a useful addition to the diets of kestrels, badgers and even eagles and herons. Foxes seem to prefer field voles to all other small mammals.

Field voles' preferred habitat is long, tussocky grass and they are rarely found anywhere else. They eat grass, make nests of it and burrow among its roots and stems. Few other species of British mammals are so restricted in their habitat, yet because permanent grassland is so widespread in Britain, especially in the uplands, there is plenty of space for these animals to survive in very large numbers. Despite this, numbers are declining, although the field vole may still be Britain's most numerous wild mammal, with a total population of around 75 million before the start of the breeding season.

Grass kingdom

Lack of grazing on grassland allows scrub and woody vegetation to spread. Without sufficient grazing activity the woody scrub becomes so dense that it shades the grass from the sun, causing it to wither. In turn, field voles suffer as their food declines and their grassy world begins to disappear.

EARS AND TEETH

Given its close association with grassland, the field vole is undoubtedly aptly named. However, its alternative name of short-tailed vole is also appropriate because its tail rarely reaches 30 per cent of the length of the head and body. The field vole's scientific name, *Microtus agrestis*, is fitting, too. It means 'small-eared [creature] of the fields', and this species has ears that are so short they barely emerge above the fur of the head.

The field vole has distinctive teeth, which have evolved to tackle grass. All voles have teeth with a zigzag pattern on their surfaces, but in the field vole this is more pronounced. It creates a lot of very sharp edges on the animals' teeth that help to shred grass – a much tougher food than the herbage consumed by bank voles.

Emerging from its grassland burrow, this field vole is taking a great risk by moving out into the open to investigate possible food. If it remains here for long, it may be snatched up by a hunting bird such as a kestrel.

FIELD VOLE FACT FILE

The greyish or dull brown fur of the field vole helps to distinguish the species from the reddish brown bank vole. The field vole lives in overgrown fields with long, rough grasses and usually remains in the vicinity of its nest.

● **NAMES**
Common names: field vole, short-tailed vole
Scientific name: *Microtus agrestis*

● **HABITAT**
Thick grassland, moorland, sand dunes, young conifer plantations and sometimes hedgerows and open woodland

● **DISTRIBUTION**
Throughout mainland Britain and on some islands; absent from Ireland and many Scottish islands, the Isles of Man, Scilly and Lundy, and the Channel Islands

● **STATUS**
Abundant where it occurs, but patchy in the lowlands; estimated 75 million individuals at the start of the breeding season

● **SIZE**
Head and body 80–135mm (3⅛–5⅜in); tail length 18–50mm (¾–2in); weight 15–50g (½–1½oz)

● **KEY FEATURES**
Normally greyish brown above, with grey belly; tail uniform pinkish brown and short, less than one-third length of head and body; face typically blunt-nosed, with small eyes and ears barely projecting beyond the fur; often squeaks if alarmed or handled; has a distinctive musky, cheesy smell

● **HABITS**
Mainly nocturnal, but often active during the day; adults compete for territory and are quick to fight

● **VOICE**
Loud squeaks, chirps and angry chattering noises when defending its small territory

● **FOOD**
Mostly grass, also other plant material, including clover, young bark and bulbs

● **BREEDING**
Up to 7 litters of 4–6 young produced March–October; gestation period 18–20 days

● **NEST**
Ball of finely shredded grass, about 10cm (4in) in diameter, situated underground or among grass roots

● **YOUNG**
Born pink and blind, weighing 2g (fraction of an ounce); weaned at 2 weeks

● **SIGNS**
Small piles of oval, green droppings about 3–4mm (⅛in) long, and tiny heaps of shredded and chewed grass, left in tunnels among grass tussocks

Newly born field voles are helpless and dependent upon their mother for food, warmth and shelter. The first litters are usually born in March or April, followed by a succession throughout the year.

Distribution map key

▓	Present all year round
☐	Not present

Fur grows inside the ears and on the upper edges so that they can hardly be seen.

Its short and rounded face has small bright eyes.

The grey-brown fur often has a yellowish tinge.

Darker above than below, the tail is short and sparsely haired.

On the other hand, if there is too much grazing – or mowing – the grass is left so short that field voles cannot find suitable cover, and sooner or later they are eaten by predators. This is exactly what has happened in many farmland and suburban areas, where cows, sheep, horses and mowing machines create a short-grass habitat unsuitable for voles.

Pockets of abundance

Once the field voles have gone from an area they are unlikely to return, because they do not travel very far, especially over open farmland or across wide roads. Therefore, despite their abundance nationally, field voles are now absent or scarce in many parts of the lowlands, leading to extremely patchy populations. Even in the uplands, sheep can graze grass right down while planting conifer plantations destroys the habitat on which the voles depend.

Field vole numbers have declined over the last 50 to 100 years as a result of increasingly efficient farming, which has found ways to utilise previously uncultivated land. In lowland areas, 'wasteland', which is ideal for field voles, has been eagerly snapped up by developers to build roads, houses,

out-of-town supermarkets and to cater for activities that leave little room for the long grass that the voles need.

Another problem has been rabbits, because these animals nibble grassland into very short, trimmed 'lawns'. Rabbit numbers have steadily increased since the disastrous crash brought about by the disease myxomatosis in the 1950s, and where they have become more numerous, the field vole has been in retreat.

Food for thought

All this bodes ill for field voles, which is also bad for their predators. Although other species of small mammals may move in to take the place of field voles as the habitat changes, they are often harder to catch. Wood mice, for example, are happy to live in short grass, but are very fast on their feet and easily evade predators. Bank voles move in with scrub encroachment but again are a poor

In cold winter weather, hungry field voles may be driven to exploit unusual food sources. Abandoning its fear of open spaces and a natural aversion to climbing, this one nibbles peanuts in a bird feeder.

substitute for their grass-loving cousin because the scrub makes it harder for owls and mammalian predators to get at them. Catching field voles in open grassland is easy by comparison.

Predators that are forced to rely on species of small mammals other than the field vole for food soon find themselves spending far more energy in capturing their prey, but obtaining only the same amount of food for their trouble. An adult barn owl, for instance, might manage to sustain itself on bank voles or wood mice, but is unable to catch enough of these rodents to raise a family. This is why any efforts to conserve the barn owl, or reintroduce pine martens, must first

▲ Acute hearing and a good sense of smell enable the field vole to detect potential danger as well as sources of food. The species has a reputation for being rather short-sighted.

▶ A mature orchard full of windfall apples provides a field vole with an extra source of food in autumn and early winter. In rural areas, these opportunistic feeders may even come to feed on fruit put out on garden birdtables.

◄ A nest may be exposed when grassland is cut, but if it is quickly covered up again, the female field vole will probably not desert her young.

▲ As the young field voles grow, they become more adventurous and begin to wander away from the nest site on short forays. They encounter their parents less and less frequently as the weeks progress.

look at the condition of the local environment in terms of supporting a thriving field vole population.

The many field voles that are taken by predators are soon replaced because voles are prolific breeders. The females usually produce their first young by late March or early April and continue to breed until October. They have a succession of litters (between two and seven), one after the other, throughout the summer – sometimes even during the winter. Each

litter typically comprises about four to six babies, which take just two weeks to rear. The young female voles are themselves able to breed at four weeks of age, while the males take a further two weeks to reach maturity. This means that voles born early in the season can themselves soon be breeding, contributing yet more babies to the population. Meanwhile, following a pregnancy lasting 18–20 days, their mother can have another litter, and another – and so on.

Field vole populations follow a boom and bust pattern. In some years, at about three to five-year intervals, vole numbers can build up to very high levels, followed by a population crash. These booms often occur where long grass is available in a suitable place, such as in areas that have been fenced off to plant conifers. Fencing keeps out sheep, allowing the grass to grow long and thick. Here the voles flourish, at least for a few years until their grassy habitat is succeeded by the trees,

Bright eyes and twitching nose

In the mysterious hours of twilight, a field vole emerges from its nest and scurries along the network of runways it has worn through the long grass. It sprays the path with a pungent scent as it goes.

Peering short-sightedly skywards, the vole sniffs the air for hunting birds, such as owls and kestrels.

When it picks up the scent of another vole, it pauses to decide whether to change direction or risk an aggressive confrontation.

With nose twitching, the newly emerged field vole is alert for the slightest sign of danger.

ISLAND HOME

Field voles are absent from Orkney, but a race of the European common vole, the Orkney vole (*Microtus arvalis orcadensis*), lives there. This may have been introduced by Stone Age settlers some 5400 years ago. Orkney voles probably originated from southern Europe. They were once abundant, but intensive use of farmland means that today the voles are restricted to grassy strips alongside ditches and roads and in the less suitable habitats of moorlands and bogs. The total population probably consists of fewer than one million animals.

Orkney voles build tunnels in the grass and are active during the day and night at about three-hour intervals. They usually return to a grassy nest to sleep, but may take short naps in their tunnels. They eat grass and other vegetation. The voles breed throughout the summer, producing relatively small litters. Nevertheless, high densities of animals may build up, over 250 per hectare (2½ acres) in good habitats. The young breed the year after their birth and die soon afterwards. A different race of the European common vole is found on Guernsey.

The presence of good numbers of Orkney voles on the islands' moorland enables predatory birds, notably hen harriers and short-eared owls, to breed there successfully.

▲ Although the field vole feeds mainly on the succulent lower stems of grasses, it may venture out from a field edge to sample an arable crop, especially if this is a cereal one.

which shade out the grass and the voles have to go elsewhere. Moorland vole predators, such as hen harriers and short-eared owls, prosper during this period.

Outside conifer plantations, predators generally help to suppress the field vole's cycles of abundance. In good vole years, owls and birds of prey benefit and often manage to rear more young themselves. Where there are insufficient predators, however, vole numbers reach plague proportions and the animals may inflict considerable damage on the vegetation.

During the 1890s and again in the 1920s and 1930s there were many instances of 'vole plagues', where field voles became so numerous that they caused significant damage to farm crops and newly planted trees. Where the animals had been forced out of their preferred habitat by sheer pressure of numbers, they invaded other habitats and even damaged orchard fruit trees by gnawing at the bark.

Vole behaviour

Field voles are aggressive little creatures, especially the adult males, which defend exclusive territories against rivals. Adult females fiercely defend their nests and young. However, they are tolerant of their own offspring and juvenile females often manage to remain within their mother's territory or close by. Young males are driven out, probably by their father, and so have to find somewhere new to live. This helps to prevent the population from becoming locally inbred.

Field voles do not disperse very far, rarely travelling beyond a few hundred metres from their nest. They do not live very long either, although this is perhaps not surprising bearing in mind they are the favourite food of so many predators.

▼ Juicy blackberries are a delicious treat for this field vole and worth leaving its runways to investigate. Afterwards, it will fastidiously wash its face, whiskers and paws to clean off the sticky juice.

▲ Field voles make runs where there is just enough grass cover to prevent them being visible from above. Sometimes a vole will take a short rest in a tunnel before continuing its search for food.

◄ A vole that is slow to respond to sounds and smells that spell danger is not likely to survive for long. At periodic intervals during its daily travels, it will pause to sniff the air.

Probably fewer than 5 per cent of field voles live to be more than about 18 months old and very few survive through a second winter.

Field voles are active at all times of the day, although in summer they are mainly nocturnal, with peaks of activity around dawn and dusk. In winter, very cold nights encourage them to emerge during the day. They are often busier on wet days, too, perhaps because the creatures that hunt them prefer to remain inactive rather than suffer the rain. Field voles are relatively unaffected by wet weather, sheltered in their tunnel systems, hidden deep among the grass tussocks.

Each field vole has its own home range and generally remains within the same area throughout its adult life. Surrounded by all the grass it could possibly want, a vole does not have to travel far to find the 30g (1oz) of food it needs each day. A patch as small as 100 square metres (1000 sq ft) may be sufficient to live in, and often the home territories of several voles overlap to a considerable degree.

The ranges of adult males are about twice the size of those of females. Each male, therefore, has access to several females living nearby, but they tend to avoid each other outside the mating season. Where plenty of nutritious grass is available, numbers of voles are highest and their home ranges are small. In poorer habitats, the animals may be more thinly spread over a larger area. The best grassy habitats occur where the ground is moist, but this can mean flooding in winter. Fortunately, field voles are good swimmers and can retreat into the grass tussocks above water level and wait for the flood to subside.

Scent signals

Field voles scurry about in their labyrinth of runways and tunnels that spread among grass roots and underground. They keep in touch with each other by leaving scent markers via large sensory glands on their hips. The distinctive smell is deposited with urine and piles of oval green droppings. Other voles passing by can 'read' these signs and interpret the smells to determine who is in the vicinity.

Experiments have shown that individual voles can recognise their own species by smell, and it is likely that they can also tell the sex and breeding condition of other voles. Field voles are also quite vocal, squeaking loudly, especially during aggressive encounters. However, these noises are exactly what an owl or fox may be waiting to hear before pouncing to secure a meal.

Winter is a testing time for the field vole. The thaw after heavy snowfall may cause its burrows and tunnels to become compacted and waterlogged, forcing the animal to the surface.

WILDLIFE WATCH

Where can I see field voles?

● The field vole's world is normally invisible, buried deep among dense masses of old grass. Pulling apart grass tussocks may expose vole tunnels among the stem bases and roots. Piles of nibbled grass or oval green droppings are evidence of field voles.

● Sheets of corrugated iron or hardboard lying in grass offer shelter under which field voles like to build their nests. These are made of finely shredded grass, with tunnels leading off in different directions, and may be clearly visible if the sheet is lifted. Do not expose the nest for long and always replace the sheet carefully.

● Sometimes in winter, all may be revealed when snow melts after it has been lying on the ground for a long time. While the snow is present, the voles make new runs on top of the grass, but hidden under the snow. When the snow melts, masses of runs, burrows and nests are suddenly exposed.

The skylark

A high-flying bird of the open countryside, the skylark is well adapted for life in a treeless landscape. Its streaky brown plumage allows it to nest unseen on the ground among grassy tussocks and arable stubble.

Many people would fail to recognise a skylark if they saw one simply standing on the ground, but when the male takes to the air to perform its rhapsodic song flight its identity is beyond doubt. Rising higher and higher into the summer sky, it delivers an apparently unbroken flow of warbling, trilling notes that may last for many minutes until eventually the bird spirals back down to the ground.

Camouflaged plumage

Visually, the skylark is an inconspicuous creature. Slightly smaller than a starling, it has rather drab brown, fawn and black streaked plumage, relieved only by the white outer tail feathers and a narrow whitish trailing edge to the wings. On the bare earth of arable farmland, the streaky coloration provides almost perfect camouflage, and the bird is often hard to see until it moves. It does have a few distinctive features, however, including an unusually long hind claw and a short, spiky crest on its head, which becomes erect when the bird is excited or alarmed.

Its bill is the typically strong, conical bill of a seed-eater, and much of its diet consists of seeds and grain. It also eats insects in summer and relies on them to provide the protein required by its growing young in the breeding season. The skylark forages almost exclusively on the ground, where it is easily hidden by low-growing vegetation, such as grass or young crops. Outside the breeding season it may feed in large flocks of a hundred or more, but still remain almost invisible.

Originally a bird of dry, treeless steppe, the skylark has adapted to a variety of open habitats including arable land, rough pasture, salt marsh, sand dunes and even neglected grassland in urban areas. As a result it is among the most widespread of all breeding birds in the British Isles, and the only places from which it is missing are the highest

On farmland or downland, in a shallow depression, the female skylark builds her nest of grass. The birds may raise two or more broods during the summer.

DID YOU KNOW?

In the past, thousands of downland skylarks were netted and sold in London markets for food, and were regularly cooked in pies. Today this is illegal in Britain, but they are still hunted in France where they are used to make lark pâté. Fortunately, not many larks are required for this dish, the ingredients of which are supposed to comprise one skylark to one cow!

summits in Scotland, Ireland and Wales and the Isle of Lewis. It does not require trees for feeding or breeding, and it has overcome the lack of song posts by singing in the sky, often at great heights. Delivered in flight, the song carries remarkably well, and probably farther than it would if performed from a perch.

SKYLARK FACT FILE

The skylark is better known for its song than its appearance, especially as it is often concealed on the ground when feeding or at the nest. Even the song may seem to come from an empty sky, as the singing males often fly so high that they are out of sight.

● NAMES
Common name: skylark
Scientific name: *Alauda arvensis*

● HABITAT
Open grassland, arable land, dunes and salt marsh, plus rough ground in built-up areas

● DISTRIBUTION
Throughout British Isles breeding almost everywhere apart from a few upland areas in Scotland, Isle of Lewis, Ireland and Wales

● STATUS
Huge decline over past 30 years – probably fewer than a million breeding pairs left in Britain

● SIZE
Length 18–19cm (7–7½in); weight 33–45g (1–1½oz)

● KEY FEATURES:
A medium-sized songbird; body long and stout, legs, wings and tail quite long; plumage rich but pale chestnut brown with dark streaks; underparts streaked above, pale below; tail with long white outer feathers; wings have pale trailing edges; bill strong; short crest, pale eye-ring and eyebrow stripe

● HABITS
Terrestrial nester and feeder; high-altitude song flight; most populations sedentary during winter, but upland birds move to lower ground; some migrants visit Britain in winter

● VOICE
Loud, melodious song comprising a sustained tinkling, lilting series of high-pitched warbles and trills; apparently unbroken flow, but generally in bursts lasting 3–5 minutes, occasionally as long as 20 minutes; song flight up to one hour in duration; calls varied, most common an abrupt '*tit-terrreep*'

● FOOD
Plant and animal material taken from the ground throughout the year; mainly seeds, cereal grain and leaves in winter and spring; in summer, also many insects, which are important for feeding nestlings

● BREEDING
Eggs first laid late April; pair often has 2 and sometimes 3 or even 4 broods; last young to hatch fledge in early September

● NEST
Cup of grass lined with fine grasses or animal hair, in shallow depression on the ground, generally concealed in short vegetation, often by side of grass tussock

● EGGS.
Dull whitish, heavily spotted with brown or grey; clutch generally 3–4, occasionally 5, incubated for 11 days by female

● YOUNG
Nestlings hatch with tufts of long down on the head and back; juveniles have speckled, scaly looking upperparts and shorter tails than adults; young leave nest at 8–10 days old, fledge at 18–21 days

Woven from coarse grass and roots, the nest is lined with finer grasses and hair. The clutch of pale eggs is hidden from predators by a tussock of grass or a crop plant.

Usually sleeked back to the head, the short spiky crest becomes prominent when the bird is excited.

A light-coloured supercilium and eye-ring give the face a pale appearance.

Variable reddish to greyish brown feathers on the back have broad blackish brown streaks.

Stout and conical, the bill is used to crack seeds.

Heavily streaked with brown, the breast contrasts with the pale buff underparts.

Distribution map key

Present all year round

Present only during summer months

White outer tail feathers are noticeable in flight.

The long rear claw provides extra balance on the ground.

PROTECTED!

It has been illegal to catch skylarks in the British Isles since 1931, and the bird is now fully protected under the Wildlife and Countryside Act, 1981.

SKYLARK CALENDAR

JANUARY • FEBRUARY

Flocks of skylarks are at their largest in mid-winter. They may be concentrated in areas where snow has been blown off the winter fields, enabling the birds to get at leaves, grain and seeds.

MARCH • APRIL

The glorious song of the males is truly memorable as skylarks start to set up breeding territories, pair up and lay their first clutches of eggs. The young hatch after around 11 days.

MAY • JUNE

The breeding season reaches its peak as the birds rear second broods. The adults forage busily to feed their hungry young. Males continue to confirm their territories with song.

JULY • AUGUST

All is quiet in August as the breeding season ends and the birds begin to moult. Young birds lose their soft, spotty plumage and adults replace tattered, worn-out feathers.

SEPTEMBER • OCTOBER

With the cooling temperatures of autumn, skylarks use perches as they start to gather in flocks. Upland breeders move to lower ground for the winter.

NOVEMBER • DECEMBER

Resident skylarks are joined by migrants from northern Europe around suitable feeding areas, particularly on coastal marshes and farmland with winter stubbles and fallow fields.

Ground feeder

The skylark spends much of its time on the ground, busily pecking at apparently bare earth, looking for any tiny weed seeds that are lying dormant in the soil. Skylarks also forage for spilt grain and, in summer, for insects to feed their young.

A skylark walks sedately over uneven ground, ready to hop over any obstacles in its way, intent on finding food.

It relies on the camouflage provided by its streaky plumage to protect it from predators. When danger threatens the skylark raises its crest in alarm.

Holding its sturdy, plump body low, with its legs bent ready for flight, the skylark cautiously continues its search for seeds, looking around at intervals.

Territorial display

The male's song flight advertises the fact that the territory holder is well in control. Each male usually sings within 60m (200ft) of the nesting site – both around and above it – but territory sizes vary. In some areas with plentiful food, skylark territories are very small and tightly packed, while in others the range used by each pair will be very much bigger, and overlap with areas used by several neighbouring pairs.

The song also serves to reinforce the pair bond, between the male and female, so they remain together throughout the breeding season. If they breed successfully and both birds survive the winter, they may pair up again the following year. Such long-term pairings help the birds make the most of the available food and they work together to provide for their nestlings.

Lark rise

The serenade of the skylark is familar to most people, but many will not have enjoyed the wonderful experience of 'lark rise' because it occurs as the first glow of dawn breaks the darkness. It is best heard in open country, away from thick hedges or small woods, which harbour other birds, such as robins and blackbirds. These also start singing at dawn, and the skylarks will be heard most clearly where they have the air to themselves. At first all is silent, then suddenly a male skylark will take off for the first song of the day. As soon as the first bird sings others start their flights, and their voices can be heard from every direction. The closest bird gives a distinct individual song, while the

rest merge into a seamless symphony. Since skylark territories may be as small as a couple of hectares (5 acres), some 20, 30 or even 40 singing birds may be audible from one place. A dozen skylarks may be audible at the same location a few hours later, but then they will be competing with other birds, as well as a cacophony of distracting noises, such as farm machinery and aircraft.

Song flight

The start of the song flight is quite prosaic. The male bird simply looks up and takes off, steadily climbing into the wind. After climbing for a short time he starts to spiral upwards and sing. When he gains sufficient height, sometimes as low as 30–40m (100–130ft) but occasionally as high as 200m (650ft), he hovers and

A singing skylark 'hangs' in the air. Its long broad wings are outstretched and barely fluttering, their pale trailing edges clearly visible, along with white outer tail feathers.

The skylark usually hovers briefly before landing. Over short distances its flight appears somewhat weaving and fluttery, but over longer distances it becomes more purposeful and undulating.

Flying high

In spring and summer, the male skylark takes to the air, proclaiming ownership of his territory and impressing his mate with his loud, joyful song.

Wind direction

The steep, spiralling ascent is aided by flying into the wind to gain lift. All the time, the male gives voice to a liquid, warbling stream of song.

Rising off the ground at a steep angle, with rapid wingbeats, the skylark hovers briefly to begin its song.

On a warm day the skylark may stop high up in the sky, apparently motionless, pouring out its clear song for several minutes.

Then the bird 'parachutes' rapidly back to earth, landing close to the spot from where it took off.

WOODLARK AND SHORE LARK

The woodlark, *Lullula arborea*, is paler and smaller than the more familiar skylark, with a short, square tail and a striking, liquid '*lit-loo-eet*' call. It favours areas of scrubby heath with scattered large trees. Its song is a beautiful, soft, melodious series of fluting phrases, given from the ground, from a perch or in flight. The bird tends to sing while climbing and is silent as it loses height, only to ascend and sing again.

Once widespread throughout much of Wales and southern Britain, the woodlark dwindled in numbers and declined rapidly from the 1950s, reaching a low of fewer than 250 pairs in the early 1980s. This has been reversed and there are now twice that number of birds breeding in Breckland, on the borders of Norfolk and Suffolk. Woodlarks are also doing well in other areas, such as Devon, the New Forest, the Surrey and Suffolk heathlands and Nottinghamshire. They owe this revival to careful management of plantation habitats, since ensuring the survival of patches of open ground within plantations enables woodlarks to breed in them for several years after the trees have been planted. They have also benefited from earlier springs and may lay eggs in mid-March, continuing to breed until mid-September.

A scarce but regular winter visitor to Britain is the shore lark from the Scandinavian mountains. This pinkish brown bird has a yellow face and throat and a black bib, mask and crown, from which tufts of black feathers form little 'horns' in the breeding season, most obvious in males. From 200 to more than 1000 birds winter in Britain. They are often found in mixed flocks with snow buntings and Lapland buntings, on salt marshes and sand dunes along the east coast and the Dee estuary in Cheshire and north Wales.

◀ Throughout the spring and summer the woodlark forages to feed its hungry brood, busily pecking up fat insects and spiders. Outside the breeding season it feeds mainly on seeds.

▲ The shore lark is smaller and slimmer than the skylark, with a distinctive head pattern of black and yellow. The best way to spot one is to listen for a shrill, rather piping '*teseee-it*'.

▶ Woodlarks prefer dry heathland or downland, with long grass for nesting and short grass for feeding. The first brood of three to four chicks is raised from mid-March onwards.

circles slowly. The content of the song is very varied, and it is not unusual for skylarks to mimic other local species. They may imitate waders in marshland areas, and linnets in farmland. The flight may last for less than half a minute or, exceptionally, for around 20. The bird then descends in slow spirals, his wings held extended and motionless. He sometimes continues to sing while gliding down to land, usually stopping just before reaching the ground, when he suddenly folds his wings and drops into cover.

Ground cover

Skylarks nest on the ground, in the open or sometimes sheltered among short grass or growing crops. The nest is lined with

Inconspicuous plumage allows the female skylark to blend in with the surroundings while she is sitting on her eggs. The male does not help with incubation.

grass and built in a shallow hollow, often sheltered by a tussock of grass or, rarely, protected by a rampart of small stones. In late March to early May, the female lays between three and five eggs, which are pale and heavily speckled with brown and grey.

The newly hatched nestlings have tufts of long down that help conceal them from predators, such as foxes, stoats, weasels, crows and magpies. They leave the nest after just eight or 10 days, hiding singly among surrounding thick ground cover and usually returning to the nest only at night. During this time they develop a speckled, scaly-looking plumage, but they do not fly properly until they are about three weeks old. Up until then they are still fed by their parents. The adult birds are very careful not to alert predators to the nest or the whereabouts of the young. They never fly directly to them, but land some distance away and approach on foot.

When disturbed, a skylark stands bolt upright and raises its well-streaked crest. This is most unlike the usual creeping posture that it adopts when feeding on weed seeds lying on the ground.

Steep decline

The marked reduction in skylark numbers in recent decades has several causes. For instance, during particularly long, cold winter spells many birds will die, residents as well as those driven to the British Isles to escape harsh weather in northern Europe.

More significant, though, is the skylark's shrinking habitat. Skylarks breed on open land, particularly arable farmland, and more than half the breeding population has been lost over the last 30 years as agriculture has become more intensive. Autumn sowing of crops reduces the stubbles that provide food for the birds in winter, and by spring the crops are so tall and thick that skylarks are unable to nest among them. They often resort to nesting on wheel tracks or 'tramlines' through the crop that are created by farm machinery, and are either crushed or taken by predators, which can find them easily. Herbicides reduce the weeds in the crop, depriving insects of their foodplants and the nestlings of their insect food. Insects may be scarce anyway because of the use of pesticides.

Farm tracks and rough corners are very important for skylarks. In the long term, a return to less intensive mixed and organic farming methods may reverse the skylark's decline.

ARTFUL SONG

The quality of the skylark's song was well caught by the poet George Meredith:

He drops the silver chain of sound,
Of many links without a break.

The skylark – and Meredith's poem – were also the inspiration for 'The Lark Ascending' by Ralph Vaughan Williams, a much-loved musical celebration of the soaring beauty of the song. Many other musicians have also been inspired by the level of impromptu variation within each bird's song. Indeed, the same sequence of song phrases may not be repeated for an hour or more.

▼ Insects are particularly important to the skylark in summer when it has young to feed. An adult collects as many insects as it can cram in its bill and then calls the young to come out from their hiding places to eat.

► The skylark frequently builds its nest in an existing depression in the ground, such as a cow's hoof print. The nestlings' soft brown plumage provides effective camouflage.

WILDLIFE WATCH

How can I see skylarks?

● Among the most widespread of British birds, skylarks can be found almost anywhere in summer, from the Scottish Highlands to the wide, open spaces of the east coast saltings just above the high-tide line.

● Skylarks' main requirement is access to crop and weed seeds. This means that the highest numbers of these birds are found on arable land where their food is easy to find. Farmland with light soils is preferred because some of the crops are sown in the spring and do not grow too densely for the birds to nest.

● Pasture land with cultivated grasses is not good for skylarks, but the edges of lowland or upland pasture with plenty of weeds and tussocks can support many breeding pairs.

● During the winter, look for flocks of skylarks on the coast, especially among sand dunes, on high saltmarsh and on coastal grazing land. They may also be seen on farmland with winter stubbles. Golf courses can be good places to look.

● In summer, a car can be used as a hide to watch the birds gathering food and then disappearing into the longer grass to feed their broods.

● Newly felled conifer plantations are used by nesting woodlarks. These birds are abundant in Thetford Forest. They will return to the same areas of heathland year after year. For information, contact the Royal Society for the Protection of Birds (telephone 01767 680551), the Forestry Commission Office (telephone 01313 340303) or the Wildlife Trust (telephone 08700 367711).

The lapwing

Flamboyantly flashing wings and shrill calls make the lapwing easily identifiable in flight. On the ground, however, parent birds quietly shelter their nestlings from summer rain and cautiously lead them to patches of long, damp grass to feed.

A bird of open countryside, the lapwing is known by many different old country names. Some of these describe its appearance and even its nature, such as green plover, for the bird is indeed a plover with dark metallic green plumage on its back, wings and tail. Others – including the name lapwing and the archaic flopwing – describe its distinctive, floppy-winged flight style. Most of the old names, however, are derived from the bird's calls or springtime song, and these include names such as peewit, piewipe, peasiewheep, teuchit and even bullock-a-week.

A big flock of lapwings makes a wonderful sight when the birds take to the air, and the males are well known for their spectacular aerial displays. In the past, however, lapwings were best known for their eggs. Until the 1960s, these were regularly and legally collected in large numbers to be sold as a gourmet delicacy, rather like quail's eggs today. Served in their shells in moss-lined baskets, they were valued as much for their attractive appearance as their taste. Now that the lapwing is on the decline as a breeding bird in Britain, 'plover's eggs' can be collected only at certain times under special licence, and such licences are granted rarely.

Seasoned travellers

In Spain, the lapwing is known as *avefria* – the bird of the frosts – because really large numbers arrive on Spanish soil only in winter when the weather is especially cold. In Britain, snowstorms spreading south may provoke mass movements of lapwings, which can be seen steadily flapping their way south and west against leaden skies, traversing town and country alike as they migrate to places with milder winter climates.

INCREDIBLE JOURNEYS

Some of the most exceptional long-distance recoveries of British-ringed lapwings date from unusually cold spells, such as the winter of 1962–3. One example occurred in December 1927 when a lapwing ringed in Britain the previous summer turned up with a large flock in Newfoundland. An anticyclone established over Scandinavia caused temperatures to plummet, and the freezing conditions forced the birds to seek warmer climes.

Meteorological data suggests that the flock probably took off during a south-westerly gale, missed the north coast of Ireland and kept going. This would normally have been a journey to oblivion, but a huge area of low pressure just east of Newfoundland created an exceptionally strong wind blowing from the east. Caught up in the gale, the birds were swept across the Atlantic with the help of an 80km/h (50mph) tailwind. All they had to do was head west at their normal flight speed, and the journey of 3220km (2000 miles) would have taken just a day and a half.

Calling all the while, a displaying male lapwing rises high above his nesting territory before tumbling out of the sky in a headlong dive.

LAPWING FACT FILE

Strikingly crested and boldly patterned, the lapwing looks black and white from a distance, but at close range its metallic green upper plumage becomes clearer. The dramatic plunging display flight of the male birds is a common sight in spring.

● NAMES
Common names: lapwing, northern lapwing; old names include green plover, peewit, piewipe, peasiewheep, teuchit and flopwing
Scientific name: *Vanellus vanellus*

● HABITAT
Arable farmland, pasture, wetlands, salt marsh, estuaries; also uplands in summer

● DISTRIBUTION
Breeds throughout British Isles except far south-west of Britain and Ireland, the London area and north-west Scottish Highlands

● STATUS
Breeding population has declined by more than 30% over past 30 years, to 200,000–250,000 pairs; winter influx of eastern birds boosts population to about 2 million pairs

● SIZE
Length 28–31cm (11–12½in); weight 150–300g (5½–10½oz)

● KEY FEATURES
Iridescent green back and tail; male has iridescent blue on 'shoulders'; underparts white with bright chestnut under tail; legs dark pinkish, bill black; young have pale tips to back feathers; summer male has much more black on face than female

● HABITS
Feeds, roosts and nests on the ground; flies in large flocks with distinctive floppy wingbeats

● VOICE
Main calls resemble country name *'peewit'* or *'peet'*, harsher and more insistent when alarmed; spring song of male is *'chair-weedle-weep, ee-weep, ee-weep'*, given in tumbling display flight over territory with loud humming from stiff flight feathers

● FOOD
Beetles, flies, ants and other insects and larvae; molluscs, spiders, earthworms and other invertebrates; occasional small frogs and plant material

● BREEDING
First eggs laid mid-March–April; replacement clutches (if first one fails) May–June

● NEST
Simple scrape on bare ground, often on slight rise so incubating bird can see surroundings

● EGGS
3–5 (usually 4) eggs with buff stone coloured background and bold dark blotches and scribbles; incubation takes around 4 weeks

● YOUNG
Leave the scrape almost immediately after hatching, cared for by both parents; fledge after 35–40 days

A shallow scrape barely lined with plant material serves as a nest for the lapwing. Responsibility for incubation is shared by both parents, although the female takes the leading role.

Longer in males than females, the distinctive crest is at its longest in the breeding season.

The shimmering green iridescence of the back feathers contrasts boldly with the clean white underparts.

Distribution map key

■ Present all year round

▢ Present during summer months

▢ Present during winter months

▢ Not present

GOLDEN PLOVER

In the breeding season, the golden plover (*Pluvialis apricaria*) is a bird of upland moors, occurring in Scotland, parts of northern England, Wales, Dartmoor and western Ireland from mid-April all through May. In winter, however, it often joins lapwing flocks. In many areas the traditional wintering sites of the two species coincide, and the slightly smaller golden plover is regularly seen among lapwings from autumn to spring. They are also found together on migration, the golden plover's spangled summer and autumn plumage making it stand out.

Golden plovers are surprisingly mobile. Individuals from the Pacific sometimes turn up in Britain as vagrants, and they breed right around the Arctic Circle on moorland and tundra. Recently, birds once believed to be subspecies of golden plover have been reclassified as distinct species, such as the Pacific golden plover (*Pluvialis fulvia*) and the American golden plover (*Pluvialis dominica*). On the other hand, the two forms that breed and winter in Britain are now categorised as the same species. The type that used to be called *'altifrons'* has more contrasting black and white on the plumage and was once considered to be a northern race. However, detailed study has shown that, although these birds are more numerous in the north, they occur in all populations along with birds that have especially mottled plumage.

Some golden plovers are long-distance migrants. Relatively few are ringed, but the records clearly show that they fly from Iceland to Britain and Ireland, and as far as Spain, Portugal and Morocco. Some British birds venture abroad, but most move to the milder regions of southern and western Britain. Some Scandinavian birds winter in Britain, too, but most of them go to France, Spain, Portugal and Morocco. Golden plovers have declined markedly in the southern parts of their European range over the last 50 years.

▲ The golden plover gets its name from its golden-spangled back. In breeding plumage its underparts are black, emphasising the white eyestripe that continues down each side of the neck.

◄ Like lapwings, golden plovers nest on the ground and are vigorous in the defence of their nesting sites. They breed on moorlands and upland pastures, but spend the winter in the lowlands.

▼ Between May and June, the female golden plover lays four pale green or olive eggs, which are incubated by both parents for around four weeks. The eggs are mottled with darker markings and are hard to see among rough moorland vegetation.

Mixed flocks of lapwings and golden plovers occur in traditional lowland sites in winter. Both favour wet ground, so large flocks often accumulate around estuaries, floodplains and gravel pits.

These cold-weather movements are remarkable enough, but bird-ringing evidence shows that young lapwings reared in western Europe sometimes pair up with birds from far to the east, and travel with them to breed far away in eastern Europe or even Asia. As a result of this, up to a quarter of breeding-season recoveries of birds ringed as nestlings in Europe take place more than 300km (180 miles) from the ringing site, and 15 per cent are found more than 1000km (620 miles) away. The current record holders are two lapwings originally ringed in western France and Italy that were recovered in western Siberia, having travelled 5850km (3635 miles) and 5500km (3420 miles) respectively.

Such 'abmigrations' – flights in the opposite direction to the usual route – ensure that the birds interbreed over a large area, so it is not surprising that lapwings are alike throughout their range. However, most British and Irish lapwings travel less than 100km (60 miles), and usually return to the sites where they hatched when they are ready to breed.

Flashing wings

When the lapwing is flying, the broad tips of its large wings make an eye-catching pattern as the dark upper side flashes alternately with the white underwings and body. Male lapwings exploit this to increase the impact of their tumbling aerial display.

The black chest band makes a stark contrast with the white breast and underwing coverts, while the orange vent and whitish outer tips of the primary feathers also show in flight.

LAPWING CALENDAR

JANUARY ● FEBRUARY

The extent of migration to southerly estuaries and coasts depends on the severity of the winter. In mild years, birds will return to southern breeding grounds by the end of February.

MARCH ● APRIL

Nests are scraped and eggs laid, and sometimes lost, in most southern territories. However, birds that nest on uplands in the north may not yet have reached their breeding territories.

MAY ● JUNE

All over the country, chicks are being reared on marshes and farmland. The first migrants arrive across the North Sea from central Europe. The earliest to arrive are probably failed breeders.

JULY ● AUGUST

Flocks of young birds and adults form, although some pairs are still breeding. These late breeders probably lost their first broods, and were forced to lay replacement clutches.

SEPTEMBER ● OCTOBER

Breeding over, the birds gather in large flocks on traditional feeding sites where plenty of invertebrates are available to eat. These are often on pesticide-free farmland and marshes.

NOVEMBER ● DECEMBER

The onset of cold weather can prompt large-scale southward movements of lapwings. Very cold snaps may drive many out of the country and south into France and Spain.

Aerial manoeuvres

For much of the year male and female lapwings are almost indistinguishable, but in spring the male acquires a longer crest, a largely black face and throat, and an iridescent blue sheen on his 'shoulders'. He performs elaborate display flights over the breeding territory, tumbling, diving and swerving through the air. During the fastest dives, air rushing through the stiff flight feathers makes a vibrant throbbing sound, adding to the impact of the bird's shrill calls.

The lapwing's nest could not be simpler – a scrape in the ground with a small amount of lining. However, lapwings are very particular about where the nest is built. They favour places near water, such as wet grasslands, selecting sites that are slightly raised to reduce the risk of the nest being flooded if the water rises. Such a site also gives the incubating

▲ Lapwings fly in big, loosely bunched flocks with slow, erratic wingbeats that alternately flash the dark upperwing and white underwing plumage, creating a characteristic 'twinkling' effect.

bird a good view of approaching danger. Lapwings avoid places that have high perches nearby, because these could be used by raptors or egg thieves, such as crows. Both parents are quick to defend the nest. Birds of prey are diverted away from the site, and any ground predators that come too close, such as foxes or humans, are 'dive-bombed' to distract and disorientate them. Foxes are among the lapwing's main enemies. One study in Norfolk showed that the birds' breeding success increased almost sixfold when foxes were brought under control.

Risky journey

When the young hatch they are active and very well developed. They are able to feed themselves soon after emerging from the egg, and the parents lead them to patches of damp grassland where prey is easy to find. It is a risky journey for the young lapwings, for they are likely to be seized by predators on the way. Once feeding, they are safer and they usually stay on the same site, guarded by their parents, until they are able to fly at the age of five to six weeks. Soon after this they become independent, and by autumn they are able to make the journey to their winter quarters on lowland pastures and coasts.

▲ The young have long, sturdy legs and are soon able to find their own food, but their parents remain with them to defend them until they fledge.

▼ Superbly camouflaged by the same cryptic coloration, eggs and nestlings are hard to see among vegetation. On hearing their parents' alarm call, the tiny birds instinctively crouch motionless, becoming almost invisible.

▼ When the chicks hatch, they are covered in soft down. This is warm, but not waterproof. The parent can shelter them from heavy rain, but they soon become cold and waterlogged if they try to move about in rain-soaked vegetation.

Dwindling numbers

The lapwing has suffered a serious decline in Britain in recent decades. The reason is mainly intensive agriculture, especially the switch to autumn-sown crops, because by early spring such crops are too dense to provide good nesting sites. Undisturbed grassland is becoming scarce, especially in the south, where it is often cut for silage while the birds are still vulnerable. Besides this, pesticides and the draining of wetlands have eliminated much of the lapwing's food.

Despite this, lapwings are still numerous, especially in the north where the dramatic spectacle of displaying males is a common sight, and the bird remains an emblem of open grassland in summer.

▶ **Mobility is of crucial importance to a vulnerable young lapwing, since it has to move to better feeding grounds soon after it hatches. It must also be able to dive into cover whenever danger threatens.**

◀ **Even on wild moorland, lapwing nests may be at risk from the trampling hooves of sheep and other grazing animals. The adults remain constantly vigilant, and are fearless in confronting inquisitive ewes.**

Strutting display

The lapwing raises its slender crest whenever it wants to draw attention to itself. Lapwings with eggs in the nest, or young, often display in a similar way some distance from the scrape or feeding area to distract predators.

A male lapwing struts around the scrape he has made to serve as a nest, crest held high.

Burnet moths

As they flutter from bloom to bloom in a flower-strewn meadow, brightly coloured burnet moths make no attempt to hide. Their vivid markings are a warning to hungry birds that the moths' bodies are packed with poisons.

Dramatically coloured, day-flying burnet moths are a conspicuous feature of flowery grasslands in summer. With their glossy black bodies, red-spotted wings and clubbed antennae they are often mistaken for butterflies, but their resting posture, with their wings folded tent-like over their bodies, is characteristic of moths. Less obviously, they have a stout bristle linking their forewings and hindwings on each side. Known as the frenulum, this feature is typical of most moths, but never found in butterflies.

There are seven British species, all with the bold colours that make them so eye-catching. They spend much of their time sipping nectar from thistles, scabiouses and knapweeds, and are far less easily disturbed than the grassland butterflies that often feed alongside them. If they do fly away, they rarely travel very far, but drift in an apparently lazy way – although, like other moths, they have to beat their wings quite rapidly to keep their relatively heavy bodies aloft.

Warning colours

Burnet moths owe their confidence to poisons in their bodies that make them taste foul. The poisons are advertised by their bright red and black coloration, which serves as a warning to birds and other potential predators. Once a young bird has attempted to eat a burnet moth, it associates the bold pattern with an unpleasant experience and is unlikely to risk it a second time. The poisons may even defend burnet moths from

Britain's most common burnet moth, the six-spot is found on chalk downs and other flowery grasslands, and in woodland glades, from late June to August. The metallic sheen on its wings and the long, thin wing shape help distinguish it from a butterfly.

▼ All burnet moths fly during the day and can be very noticeable, particularly on yellow flower heads. The red underwings of this six-spot are clearly visible as it takes off.

predators that have never encountered them before. A disturbed burnet moth often exudes bad-tasting fluids from glands around its mouth, containing volatile, pungent compounds known as pyrazines that are sufficient to repel most predators. If the attack persists, fluids that contain cyanide seep from joints on the legs and thorax. The fluids do not incorporate very much of this notoriously deadly poison, but there is certainly

enough to distress the predator and make it release the moth. Meanwhile the burnet's tough, leathery skin often protects it from harm, and even if the skin is broken it will heal very quickly. Yet despite this powerful protection, burnets are still eaten by some birds, such as wheatears, and a few spiders.

The forewings of freshly emerged burnet moths usually have a greenish or bluish sheen on the dark areas, but this

▲ In May the six-spot burnet caterpillar spins itself a pale, tapering cocoon high up on a grass stem. Once complete, the silken shroud hardens and forms a protective casing for the pupa.

▲ Laid on bird's-foot trefoils in summer, the eggs of the six-spot burnet hatch into small bristly caterpillars that feed ravenously before hibernating in late autumn.

gradually wears off to leave dull black. The hindwings are normally plain red with a black border, but individuals with yellow hindwings and spots very occasionally crop up in the six-spot, five-spot, narrow-bordered five-spot and transparent burnet moths.

Plump caterpillars

Creamy white eggs are laid in batches in summer. Most species lay their eggs on low-growing legumes, especially bird's-foot trefoils and red clover, but the transparent burnet favours wild thyme. The Scotch or mountain burnet lays its eggs on crowberry, or sometimes cowberry, bilberry or heather. The plump caterpillars that emerge a few weeks later are mostly green or yellowish with numerous black dots and tufts of short hair.

After feeding for a while, the caterpillars hibernate over winter and resume feeding in spring. Some may take two years to mature. Pupation occurs in late spring. The six-spot, five-spot and narrow-bordered five-spot burnets all spin their silken, silvery or straw-coloured cocoons high up on exposed grass stems, but the others conceal their cocoons in low vegetation. When the pupa is fully developed, it cuts open the cocoon and wriggles part of the way out before the adult hauls itself free, leaving its empty pupal skin hanging from the cocoon.

▲ On the wing in July and early August, the five-spot burnet is mainly associated with damp grassland, heaths and wetlands in southern England. Its larval foodplant is greater bird's-foot trefoil.

THE BURNET FAMILY

Burnet moths belong to the family Zygaenidae. The seven British species are variable, but can be distinguished with a little practice. The six-spot burnet is the only species with six red spots on the forewing. The five-spot burnet has five red spots, the central pair of which are usually joined. The narrow-bordered five-spot burnet is similar, but the central pair of spots are usually well separated.

The Scotch or mountain burnet is very hairy, with five often very small spots on its semi-transparent wings. The spot at the base of its forewing extends as a streak along the front edge. The outer spot of the slender Scotch burnet is larger and kidney-shaped. In the New Forest burnet, the front spot of the middle pair is distinctly smaller. The transparent burnet has thinly scaled forewings, marked with three blunt red or purplish red streaks that often merge.

The narrow-bordered five-spot burnet is common in woodlands and plantations in England and Wales in June and July.

Recognising downland butterflies

Dancing among the flowers and grasses of rolling downland, butterflies sip nectar from the most colourful blooms. From the stunning Adonis blue to the subtler meadow brown, they are at their most active on warm, summer days.

The short-turf downland that covers chalk or limestone hills is home to a distinct collection of plants and insects, including many butterflies. Some, such as the meadow brown and common blue, are found all over the British Isles while others, such as the chalkhill blue and silver-spotted skipper, are restricted to specific areas of southern England.

During the last half-century butterflies generally have suffered from the increased use of pesticides. They are particularly sensitive to drifting chemical spray. Added to this, many of their breeding sites have disappeared under the plough and, as a result, some species, such as the small blue, are declining in numbers. Others, however, are finding new places to live and expanding their range and some, such as the brown argus, are even increasing in numbers.

Short grass
Plants and insects that live on downland cannot survive for long if grasses have grown tall. They need the warm conditions of short-cropped turf – taller grassland is too cold for them. Among butterflies, the blues, especially the Adonis blue, are the first to be affected when grazing is reduced or stops. The marbled white, however, with its preference for longer grasses, is more resilient and may persist until the whole area is overtaken by bushes and eventually develops into woodland.

Grazing or mowing is therefore an essential aspect of management in downland

nature reserves, such as Martin Down, Hampshire and Coombe Bissett Down, Wiltshire, that are home to these butterflies.

In warm weather, many downland butterflies are particularly active and the air may twinkle with flashes of azure as the blues flutter among the rustling grass-heads. In some areas, many butterfly species can be seen at some time during the summer. If chalkhill blues are present, the chances are that the site is untainted by agricultural chemicals, and many other species will also be present. It goes without saying that these delicate animals are rare, and should be captured only photographically.

▲ Although not restricted to chalk hills, large numbers of meadow browns inhabit the downs. The large false eyes on the forewings serve to frighten off predators, such as birds.

▶ The Adonis blue is attracted to downland with horseshoe vetch, the only plant on which it will lay its eggs.

EASY GUIDE TO SPOTTING DOWNLAND BUTTERFLIES

WHAT ARE DOWNLAND BUTTERFLIES?

● Butterflies belong to one of the largest natural orders of insects, called the Lepidoptera, which also includes moths. Most downland butterflies belong to one of four different families – the Nymphalidae (browns and fritillaries), the Pieridae (whites), the Lycaenidae (blues) and the Hesperiidae (skippers).

● A butterfly's antennae are thickened into a club at the tips. Moths generally have comb-like antennae, with the exception of the brightly coloured day-flying burnets. Their antennae gradually thicken towards the tips.

● In butterflies, the front and hind wings are not connected, but merely overlap. Moths' wings are connected by a hook-like hair near the base of each hind wing that fits into a 'catch' on the front wing, so that they can be folded against the moth's body.

● Butterflies feed through a slim extendible 'drinking straw' called a proboscis, as do moths. The proboscis can easily reach into the deep nectar-filled chambers of flowers such as knapweed and thistle – species regularly encountered on downlands.

● Some species of butterfly, notably the Lycaenidae, have an intriguing relationship with ants. The caterpillars are always attended by ants, which 'milk' them for their sweet secretions. In return the ants guard the caterpillars and take the chrysalises into their nest, protecting them until the butterfly emerges.

The grizzled skipper can be seen basking in the sun on hot days in late May or early June.

MARBLED WHITE *Melanargia galathea*

Like the meadow brown, this butterfly belongs to the family Nymphalidae. In the evening, marbled whites often retreat to communal roosts in a secluded area of long grass. The caterpillar is very pale brown or yellow, with two brown lines along its back, a yellowish line along each side and a pelt of short hairs.

● SIZE
Wingspan male 53mm (2⅛in), female 58mm (2¼in)

● FOODPLANT FOR LARVAE
Red fescue and other grasses

● CHRYSALIS
Plump, whitish brown, tinged pinkish; lies loose among grass tussocks, or beneath soil or moss

● ADULT SEASON
June–mid-August

● HABITAT
Mostly on downlands, also on coastal grassland, roadside verges, railway embankments and wasteground

● DISTRIBUTION
Most common in south-west England but scattered as far north as Yorkshire; almost absent from Wales

A male marbled white shows its distinctive upperwing pattern. This species is increasing in numbers and expanding its range.

Underwing pattern a duller version of that seen on upperwings

Upperwings have black markings on a background of white to pale cream

MEADOW BROWN *Maniola jurtina*

The orange patch on the forewing of the female is much larger than that of the male, as is the black eyespot. One or two white spots may appear within the black eyespot, but this varies. The bright green caterpillar often has a darker line down the back and whitish stripes on each side, but is very variable.

● SIZE
Wingspan male 40–50mm (1½–2in), female 42–60mm (1¾–2⅜in)

● FOODPLANT FOR LARVAE
Fine-leaved grasses

● CHRYSALIS
Pale green above, darker below; usually found among grass stems or dead vegetation

● ADULT SEASON
June–October

● HABITAT
Downland, grassy woodland rides, disused railway lines, heaths, roadsides, riverbanks, hay meadows, wasteground, parks and gardens

● DISTRIBUTION
Occurs throughout the British Isles; probably the most common butterfly in most years

The male meadow brown is not so brightly coloured as the female, an unusual feature among butterflies.

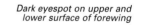

Dark eyespot on upper and lower surface of forewing

Hind wings subtly marked and marbled with grey-brown and yellowish brown

DARK GREEN FRITILLARY *Argynnis aglaja*

This stately butterfly is a strong, fast flyer. It often pauses on thistle or knapweed flowers to feed. The undersides of the hind wings are marked with silver spots on a brown background heavily suffused with green. The spiny caterpillar is mainly black, with a yellow line down the middle of its back.

- **SIZE**
Wingspan male 63mm (2½in), female 69mm (2¾in)

- **FOODPLANT FOR LARVAE**
Violets, mainly common dog-violet

- **CHRYSALIS**
Glossy black, except for the body which is dark reddish brown; hangs loosely enclosed in a tent-like cocoon of silk and grass leaves

- **ADULT SEASON**
June–August

- **HABITAT**
Open areas such as lightly grazed downs, other flower-rich grassland, coastal areas and grassy moorland

- **DISTRIBUTION**
Scattered over the whole of the British Isles except for some of the Scottish islands

The dark green fritillary can often be seen on thistles. In wetter areas in the north and west, it also feeds on marsh violets.

Upperwings a rich orange-brown patterned with dark spots, but paler in females, especially near edges

Green coloration only on the underside of the hind wings

SMALL BLUE *Cupido minimus*

The smallest butterfly resident in the British Isles, the small blue does not fly much but tends to loiter in the grass. The female is a plain dark grey-brown but in the male this is suffused with a bluish sheen. The underside is silvery grey, with a scattering of small black spots. The caterpillar is pale yellow and stripey.

- **SIZE**
Wingspan 18–27mm (¾–1in)

- **FOODPLANT FOR LARVAE**
Kidney vetch

- **CHRYSALIS**
Pale brownish, speckled with a line of blackish dots along each side; remains hidden beneath vegetation

- **ADULT SEASON**
Late May–June; second brood in August in south

- **HABITAT**
Chalk downlands, abandoned chalk and limestone quarries; sometimes beside roads cut through chalk

- **DISTRIBUTION**
Scattered widely over most of British Isles but absent from much of Scotland and most of the northern half of Ireland; main strongholds are in southern England; generally declining

Small blues often sunbathe on grasses in the morning sunshine. They seldom stray far from the clumps of kidney vetch on which they lay their eggs.

Underwings uniform silvery grey marked with distinct black spots

Upperwings of male are fringed with white and have a variable degree of blue sheen at the wing bases

BROWN ARGUS *Agricia agrestis*

Rows of bright orange spots occur down the sides of the wings of this dark brown butterfly. The adult, which is not a strong flyer, feeds low down on flowers such as common rock-rose and bird's-foot trefoil. The caterpillar is greenish, with a pinkish line down the middle of its back and a whitish line down each side.

- **SIZE**
Wingspan 25–31mm (1–1¼in)

- **FOODPLANT FOR LARVAE**
Common rock-rose

- **CHRYSALIS**
Pale greenish yellow, with pinkish stripe; hidden at the base of the foodplant among dead vegetation

- **ADULT SEASON**
May–June; second brood August

- **HABITAT**
Chalk and limestone downland and increasingly found on sand dunes, grassy coastal cliff-tops, roadside verges and woodland edges

- **DISTRIBUTION**
Southern England up to the north Midlands and Wales; expanding its range

Curiously, courting males are said to smell strongly of chocolate. This species is often seen roosting or flying in groups.

Underwing pattern similar to that of the female common blue, but spots on the forewing do not extend as close to the body

Orange spots on sooty brown upperwings are usually larger in the female and much more conspicuous than those seen on the female common blue

COMMON BLUE   *Polyommatus icarus*

Only the male has bright blue upperwings. The female is darkish brown, with varying amounts of blue and a row of orange spots near the outer wing edges. The wings of both sexes have a white border, into which the dark wing veins do not extend. The caterpillar is green with a darker green line down its back.

● **SIZE**
Wingspan 29–36mm (1⅛–1½in)

● **FOODPLANT FOR LARVAE**
Clovers, black medick, rest-harrows and trefoils

● **CHRYSALIS**
Green; lies at base of foodplant, attended by ants

● **ADULT SEASON**
May–September, in two broods, plus a small third brood

● **HABITAT**
Grassy places wherever the foodplants grow, even on regularly mown verges and golf courses; very common on downland

● **DISTRIBUTION**
All over the British Isles; vulnerable to loss of habitat

The common blue is mostly found on its larvae's foodplants, all of which belong to the pea family.

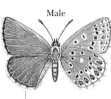

Male

Underwings of both sexes are grey-brown with dark spots bordered with white; orange spots occur at the wing margins

Upperwings have a clear white border

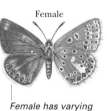

Female

Female has varying amount of blue on upperwings

CHALKHILL BLUE   *Polyommatus coridon*

Larger and paler than the common blue, with which it often flies, the male has a broad black band along the outer sides of its wings. Dark veins extend into the white wing margins. The female is mainly dark brown. The bright green caterpillar has two yellow bands down its back and a double stripe along each side.

● **SIZE**
Wingspan 33–40mm (1¼–1½in)

● **FOODPLANT FOR LARVAE**
Horseshoe vetch

● **CHRYSALIS**
Greenish brown; as with other blues, the chrysalis is guarded by ants at or below ground level

● **ADULT SEASON**
July–mid-September

● **HABITAT**
Chalk and limestone downlands and old quarries; prefers south or west-facing slopes and short turf

● **DISTRIBUTION**
Almost exclusive to downlands in an area south of a line drawn from the Severn to the Wash; not present in Wales, Scotland or Ireland

Chalkhill blues feed on the nectar from many wild flowers and are also attracted to dung.

Male

Underwings pale grey-brown marked with white-bordered black spots and an arc of orange spots on the edge of the hind wing

Male's pale blue upperwings can look almost milky white in strong sunlight

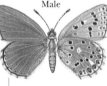

Female

Upperwings of female brown with reddish and black spots, bordered with white, along the margins

Wing bases show a hint of blue

ADONIS BLUE   *Polyommatus bellargus*

Brightly coloured wings are the male's most noticeable feature. They lack the broad black margin of the chalkhill blue, but are similar in the way the dark veins extend into the white margins. The female is usually brown, suffused with varying amounts of blue. The caterpillar is dark green with yellow stripes.

● **SIZE**
Wingspan 30–40mm (1¼–1½in)

● **FOODPLANT FOR LARVAE**
Horseshoe vetch

● **CHRYSALIS**
Greenish brown; lies on or just under the soil in a flimsy cocoon, guarded by ants

● **ADULT SEASON**
Mid-May–mid-June and again in early August–mid-September

● **HABITAT**
Downland and old chalk pits or quarries

● **DISTRIBUTION**
Restricted to a few counties in southern England, formerly more widespread

Named after the god of masculine beauty, the Adonis blue is the most vividly coloured British blue.

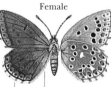

Male

Underwing grey-brown marked with white-bordered black spots

White border to male's blue upperwings broken by dark veins

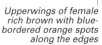

Female

Upperwings of female rich brown with blue-bordered orange spots along the edges

Blue appears at wing bases

DINGY SKIPPER   *Erynnis tages*

On warm summer evenings, the dingy skipper can be found sleeping on a dead brown flower head with its wings curved around, their upper surfaces exposed, rather like a moth. The yellowish green caterpillar has a dark, purplish brown head. It feeds mainly after dark.

● **SIZE**
Wingspan 27–34mm (1–1⅜in)

● **FOODPLANT FOR LARVAE**
Common bird's-foot trefoil

● **CHRYSALIS**
Green and brown; rests within a tent made from leaves of foodplant

● **ADULT SEASON**
May–June; in hot summers there may be a small second brood in the south in August

● **HABITAT**
Chalk downland but also other areas of short grass, woodland clearings, railway verges and wasteground

● **DISTRIBUTION**
Widespread but declining in England and rarer in the north; some in Wales; very rare in Scotland and restricted to western fringes of Ireland

A very fast-flying butterfly, the dingy skipper often stops to rest, spending long periods basking in the sunshine.

Underwings brown, often with a subtle orange wash

Brown upperwings, marbled with grey, have dark-brown markings

GRIZZLED SKIPPER   *Pyrgus malvae*

This skipper is easy to identify by its brown-and-white markings and grey (or 'grizzled') hairs. Its swift and darting flight makes this butterfly difficult to follow, but on warm days it basks on bare ground. The pale green caterpillar has a black head and is covered with short white hairs.

● **SIZE**
Wingspan 23–29mm (⅞–1⅛in)

● **FOODPLANT FOR LARVAE**
Wild strawberry, bramble, raspberry, cinquefoils, tormentil, agrimony

● **CHRYSALIS**
Light brown, marked with black along the back and sides and with deep reddish bristles on the head and sides; found near the ground in a loose silken tent

● **ADULT SEASON**
April–June

● **HABITAT**
Chalk downland, and other grassy areas such as fields, railway verges, and woodland rides and borders

● **DISTRIBUTION**
Southern and central England; very few in north-east or south Wales; absent from Scotland and Ireland; generally declining

The grizzled skipper roosts at night and in dull weather with its wings raised up from its body, revealing its chequered underwings.

Underwings have yellowish tone and a pattern of white spots

Upperwings chocolate brown and beautifully marked with variable pattern of pale spots

SILVER-SPOTTED SKIPPER   *Hesperia comma*

The upperwings of this species resemble those of the large skipper but the underwings are unmistakable with large silver spots on a greenish background colour. The adult flies rapidly in warm weather and often feeds on thistles or knapweeds. The caterpillar is dark olive green with a black head.

● **SIZE**
Wingspan male 29–34mm (1⅛–1⅜in), female 32–37mm (1¼–1½in)

● **FOODPLANT FOR LARVAE**
Sheep's fescue

● **CHRYSALIS**
Dark greyish; hidden in a silken cocoon within a grass tussock near the ground

● **ADULT SEASON**
Late July–early September

● **HABITAT**
Open chalk downland

● **DISTRIBUTION**
Extremely limited, now found mainly on the North and South Downs and in the Chilterns; generally in decline but has recently recolonised some areas

The underwings of the silver-spotted skipper are variable, being a deeper green on some adults than others.

Underwings have silvery spots

Rich orange-brown of upperwings darkens to blackish brown around edges

The glow-worm

The female glow-worm attracts a mate by switching on a beacon in her tail as she clings to a grass stem in the darkness. The male flies directly to her, drawn instinctively by the signal.

On warm summer evenings in southern Britain, spots of eerie greenish yellow light may be seen dotted among the vegetation of grassy banks and verges. They are the mating signals of one of the strangest of all British insects, the glow-worm.

Despite its name, the glow-worm is actually a small beetle. It gets its name because the female – the sex that glows in the dark – has a wingless, flexible body, and in the past it was usual to call such creatures 'worms'. A closer look, however, reveals that the female is not remotely worm-like – at 15–18mm (⅜in) long, and with a segmented, tough-skinned body, she is more like a brown woodlouse than a worm. The male is dark brown or almost black, and 10–12mm (⅛in) long, with strong wing cases that clearly identify him as a beetle. In both sexes the front of the body extends over the head like a hard, semi-transparent helmet.

Unerring males

The female glow-worm has evolved her ability to glow as a means of attracting a male. At dusk she emerges from her refuge and starts to glow in the gloom. Any males in the neighbourhood are

▲ While the winged male glow-worm (on the right) is conventionally beetle-like, the female looks more like an overgrown larva.

LIGHT WITHOUT HEAT

At all stages in the glow-worm's life cycle it can emit light – even in the egg – but the adult female is mostly responsible. The light comes from pale patches under the last three segments of her abdomen. This region is packed with luciferin, a substance that produces light through a chemical reaction involving its oxidation by an enzyme called luciferase. Almost all of the energy emitted by the reaction is in the form of light – hardly any is wasted in the form of heat. Tiny crystals of uric acid behind the luciferin act like mirrors, reflecting all the light out through the underside.

Oxygen is necessary for this light-producing reaction. The female can turn her beacon on and off at will by controlling the oxygen supply, which she

does via tiny air tubes. Switching on soon after dusk, she clings to a low support and turns her body so that the underside of her abdomen tip faces upwards. Then she waits for a male to see the signal. A sudden disturbance may cause her to switch off, but otherwise she glows continuously, and may even continue to glow if gently picked up.

▲ The light-emitting reaction occurs under the end of the female's abdomen and is not apparent from above.

◄ Twisting her tail around, the female displays the glowing lure to best effect.

immediately attracted – they have extra-large eyes to detect the light at long range, and home in on her with unerring accuracy. When a male is immediately above a female, he closes his wings and falls out of the air. This might seem a rather erratic way of approaching a potential mate, but the male's aim is remarkably good. Experiments have shown that more than half of the males tested managed to fall within two or three lengths of the glowing female.

The female often continues to glow while mating, but she extinguishes her light for good when she crawls away to lay her eggs. Each female scatters up to about 100 spherical yellow eggs in the turf or moss, and dies soon afterwards.

Glow-worm larvae resemble the adult females, although they are usually blacker and have pink patches along their sides. Adults rarely feed, but the larvae do little else. They prey mainly on small snails and slugs, and are often seen with their heads deep inside snail shells. They kill and liquefy the snails by injecting digestive juices into their bodies before consuming them. Feeding in this way is a messy business, but the insects clean themselves afterwards with the aid of tiny brushes protruding from the end of the abdomen.

The larvae take two years to mature, spending the winters under stones and logs in damp places. Mature larvae are up to 25mm (1in) long, and they pupate on the ground, buried in leaf debris. The new adults emerge about 10 days later.

Declining numbers

Fifty years ago a walk over a grassy hillside or along a country lane at night might reveal thousands of glowing lights in the vegetation. Today the insects are much rarer, and it is unusual to see more than a few dozen glow-worms in any one place. Loss of habitat has been a major factor in their decline – huge areas of grassland have been converted into arable land.

However, road traffic has been the worst culprit. Large glow-worm populations once existed on roadside verges, but these are now polluted by exhaust fumes and large numbers of male glow-worms are hit by cars as they fly in search of females. Many new verges have been created along motorways and other main roads, but it is unlikely that glow-worms will colonise these in the near future because of the relative immobility of the females.

Some railway embankments that are relatively quiet and free from pollution may support thriving glow-worm populations. The amazing spectacle of whole banks of living lights is, it seems, a thing of the past, but it is still possible to see glow-worms on summer evenings by searching in the right places.

▲ Glow-worm larvae are efficient hunters, specialising in eating small snails. The energy reserves they acquire at this stage see them through most of their short adult life, during which they will not feed at all.

DID YOU KNOW?

The glow-worm *Lampyris noctiluca* is one of two British species in the beetle family Lampyridae. The other has no English name. It is called *Phosphaenus hemipterus* and is an endangered species in Britain, confined to a few areas near the south coast. Both sexes have tiny wings but cannot fly, and the female has a very weak glow.

▼ Since the female glow-worm is flightless, she can devote most of her energy to egg production. The much smaller, sleeker, winged male is adapted for mobility and sensory perception, with big eyes.

▲ When the male glow-worm spreads his wings, he reveals a segmented body very like that of the female, only smaller.

WILDLIFE WATCH

Where can I see glow-worms?

● Pockets of glow-worms may be found all over England and Wales, but mainly in the chalk and limestone districts of the south, especially the Cotswolds and on the Isle of Wight. Even here, colonies are scattered.

● Look for the glowing females after nightfall from June to early August.

● The larvae of glow-worms depend on snails for food, and snails rely on lime in the soil to make their shells, so look for glow-worms in lime-rich soils.

● Grassy hillsides, country lanes, woodland clearings and railway embankments are good places in which to search.

Poppies

Combining fragile beauty with an astonishing capacity for regeneration, poppies are among the most irrepressible of all plants. The delicate petals may drop after just one day, but a healthy plant produces hundreds of blooms during the summer.

Vividly coloured, prolific and with seeds that are capable of springing up after decades of dormancy in the ground, poppies are among the great opportunists of the plant world. They belong to the family Papaveraceae, which numbers about 200 species, found mostly in northern temperate regions. Many of them are grown as garden flowers, but poppies are best known as plants of fields and roadsides.

Potent symbols
Since ancient times poppies have been familiar field companions to growing crops.

Their ability to appear from nowhere and tint whole fields red made them powerful symbols of both fertility and war. To the Romans field poppies were sacred to Ceres, goddess of the crops. Today they symbolise the carnage of two world wars. Following the 1916 Battle of the Somme, fought over the chalk farmland of northern France, countless poppies sprouted from buried seeds that had been disturbed by exploding shells. This is why they were adopted as an emblem of the dead, and why poppy wreaths are still laid at war memorials today.

Poppies have a number of distinctive features that separate them from other flowers. Their cut stems and leaves exude a distinctive milky juice, or latex, usually white but sometimes yellow. The leaves are deeply lobed and dissected, and sometimes almost fern-like. In bud the petals are flimsy and rumpled like tissue paper, and after they have opened they fall early and easily. The blooms are mostly red, but those of some species are yellow or orange, and the cultivated varieties (cultivars) of others may be mauve, purple, pink or white. The stamens are numerous and so

are the seeds in the fruit, or seed-capsule. In horned poppies the capsules split lengthways to release the seeds. In field poppies the seeds escape when shaken from pepper-pot-like pores near the top.

Toxic juices
The milky juices of poppies contain poisonous chemicals, including a variety of nitrogenous alkaloids that are, or have been, used in

Where the use of herbicides has been reduced, field poppies are becoming common again and masses of the red blooms grow wild in summer.

◄ No relation to the lesser celandine, which is a species of buttercup, greater celandine is a poisonous relative of those poppies that are found mainly in southern Britain.

► Opium poppies found growing wild are escapes from cultivation. They usually revert to a lilac-flowered form, and have distinctive waxy leaves.

▼ Poppies are among the first plants to sprout from freshly turned soil, and often appear at the sides of new roads.

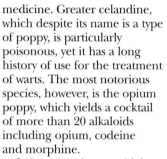

medicine. Greater celandine, which despite its name is a type of poppy, is particularly poisonous, yet it has a long history of use for the treatment of warts. The most notorious species, however, is the opium poppy, which yields a cocktail of more than 20 alkaloids including opium, codeine and morphine.

Opium poppies are widely cultivated, both legally and illegally, in warmer regions of the world, and various cultivars are popular as decorative flowers in British gardens, where the climate is too cool for the opiate alkaloids to become potent. The narcotic-free seeds are used to flavour and decorate bread and cakes.

Farm flowers

The red field poppies of farmland and waste ground are the most familiar species. They grow on a range of soils, but most commonly on chalk. Their seeds can persist for decades, especially those of the common poppy, and they germinate when conditions are favourable.

From the 1950s poppies gradually declined as the use of chemical herbicides became common. In recent years, however, more controlled use of chemicals has allowed the scarlet blooms to reappear on many farms. Fields taken out of cultivation for a year or two have briefly blazed with scarlet poppies. Wherever the soil is disturbed – perhaps during roadworks – or where a farmer has let even a strip of land go wild, there is likely to be a mass flowering of these beautiful plants.

Field and garden

British field poppies comprise four annual species. Two of them, common and long-headed poppy, are numerous, while the other two, prickly and rough poppy, are local or rare, and decreasing.

Prickly poppy is mostly found on lighter, sandy or lime-rich soils in southern and eastern England, but extends as far north as the Moray Firth. Rough poppy has a narrower distribution, mainly on chalk, and occurs in just a few areas north of a line between the Severn and Humber. In a few places, such as one site in north Cornwall, all four field poppies can be seen growing together.

Garden shirley poppies, which have flowers that are white, pink or red and are mottled or edged with white, were bred by the Reverend William Wilks in the 1880s, from a variation of the common poppy that he found growing wild in a quiet corner of his garden at Shirley, near Croydon in Surrey.

▼ Yellow horned-poppy grows on coastal shingle banks. Its very long, slender, curving seed capsules are the longest of any native British plant.

Yellow horned-poppy
Glaucium flavum

Red horned-poppy
Glaucium corniculatum

Welsh poppy
Meconopsis cambrica

POPPY FACT FILE

● **Yellow horned-poppy**
Glaucium flavum
Habitat and distribution
Coastal shingle beaches and waste ground near seashores, northwards to the Firth of Clyde
Size Up to 85cm (33½in) tall
Key features
Perennial; sap yellow; leaves deeply lobed, fleshy, silvery greyish green; flowers yellow, 6–9cm (2½–3½in) across, solitary; curved seed capsules 15–30cm (6–12in) long
Flowering time
June–September

● **Red horned-poppy**
Glaucium corniculatum
Habitat and distribution
Occasional escape from gardens, or sprouts from birdseed; native of Mediterranean region
Size Up to 85cm (33½in) tall
Key features
Very similar to the yellow horned-poppy, but has scarlet flowers and hairy seed capsules
Flowering time
June–August

● **Welsh poppy**
Meconopsis cambrica
Habitat and distribution
On and around damp, shaded rocks and walls in hilly areas of south-west England, Wales and Ireland, but established elsewhere from gardens
Size Up to 60cm (24in) tall
Key features
Perennial; sap yellow; leaves compound, deeply lobed, pale green; flowers yellow, 5–7.5cm (2–3in) across, solitary; seed capsules 2–4cm (¾–1½in) long, hairless
Flowering time
May–August

Californian poppy
Eschscholzia californica

Common poppy
Papaver rhoeas

Long-headed poppy
Papaver dubium subsp. *dubium*

Prickly poppy
Papaver argemone

Babington's poppy
Papaver dubium subsp. *lecoqii*

Rough poppy
Papaver hybridum

Opium poppy
Papaver somniferum

Atlas or Atlantic poppy
Papaver atlanticum

Greater celandine
Chelidonium majus

POPPY FACT FILE

● Californian poppy
Eschscholzia californica
Habitat and distribution
Garden escape on roadsides, waste ground, walls and seaside sandy ground; native of south-west USA
Size Up to 60cm (24in) tall
Key features
Annual; leaves greyish, feathery; flowers 2–12cm (¾–4¾in) across, orange or yellow; seed capsules up to 10cm (4in) long
Flowering time
July–September

● Common poppy
Papaver rhoeas
Habitat and distribution
The most common poppy of arable fields, waste ground, sand dunes and shingle, especially in south and east England and on chalk
Size Up to 70cm (28in) tall
Key features
Annual; leaves compound, deeply lobed; flowers scarlet, often with dark patch at each petal base, 5–10cm (2–4in) across; only British red poppy with rounded, flat-topped, hairless seed capsules
Flowering time
June–October

● Long-headed poppy
Papaver dubium subsp. *dubium*
Habitat and distribution
Arable fields and waste ground, on old walls and shingle beaches
Size Up to 60cm (24in) tall
Key features
Annual; leaves compound, deeply lobed, bluish green; flowers pinkish red, without dark patches on petals, 3–7cm (1¼–2¾in) across; smooth, club-shaped seed capsules
Flowering time
May–August

● Prickly poppy
Papaver argemone
Habitat and distribution
Local in arable fields and waste ground, mainly in south and east
Size Up to 45cm (18in) tall
Key features
Annual; compound, deeply lobed leaves; flowers pale scarlet, with dark patch at base of each petal, 5–6.5cm (2–2½in) across; bristly, club-shaped seed capsules
Flowering time
Late May–July

● Babington's poppy
Papaver dubium subsp. *lecoqii*
Habitat and distribution
Lime-rich soil in the south and east
Size Up to 60cm (24in) tall
Key features
Uncommon subspecies of long-headed poppy, with yellow sap and narrow lobes on the upper leaves
Flowering time
June–August

● Rough poppy
Papaver hybridum
Habitat and distribution
Arable fields and waste ground, mainly in southern England
Size Up to 50cm (20in) tall
Key features
Annual with compound, deeply lobed leaves; flowers pale crimson with dark patch at base of each petal, 2–5cm (¾–2in) across; almost spherical, bristly seed capsules
Flowering time
June–August

● Opium poppy
Papaver somniferum
Habitat and distribution
Garden escape of roadsides, waste ground and sometimes arable fields, especially in East Anglia where it was once a crop; probably native of Mediterranean region
Size Up to 150cm (60in) tall
Key features
Annual; leaves toothed, greyish green, waxy, usually hairless; flowers up to 5cm (2in) across, usually lilac with purple centres; seed capsules almost spherical, hairless
Flowering time
June–August

● Atlas or Atlantic poppy
Papaver atlanticum
Habitat and distribution
Garden escape increasingly established on roadsides, walls, by railways and on waste ground, mainly in south and east England; native of Morocco
Size Up to 60cm (24in) tall
Key features
Perennial with orange-red flowers 2–4cm (¾–1½in) across; club-shaped seed capsules
Flowering time
June–August

● Greater celandine
Chelidonium majus
Habitat and distribution
Hedgebanks, walls, old gardens; widespread, scarce in Scotland
Size Up to 90cm (36in) tall.
Key features
Sparse-haired perennial; sap orange; leaves with 5–9 bluntly toothed leaflets, green above, greyish green beneath; flowers rich yellow, 2–2.5cm (¾–1in) across, in clusters of 2–6. Peapod-like seed capsule, 3–5cm (1¼–2in) long
Flowering time
April–October

WILDLIFE WATCH

Where do poppies grow?

● Poppies can be found in the corners and along the edges of arable fields, on recently disturbed roadsides and waste ground and on rubbish tips. Look out for some species on coastal shingle beaches and sandy ground by the sea. Wild poppies sometimes appear in the garden.

Clovers

Whether on dry, bare ground or in damp, overgrown fields, clovers bloom throughout the summer. Individually, the flowers may be easily overlooked, but massed together on a grassy bank they create a stunning display.

Almost all the 25 species of clover that are found in the British Isles are native. These include the common red and white clovers as well as some that are less familiar. All are low-growing plants belonging to the family Fabaceae, previously known as Leguminosae, which includes the peas and beans. There are two main groups of clovers – the robust, creeping or tufted perennial plants of grasslands, and the small annual

(sometimes biennial) plants of bare or sparsely grassy places. Most flower in the summer, although some species continue into autumn.

Clover leaves are compound, each with three usually quite small, often minutely toothed, leaflets. The flowers are typically massed in spherical, egg-shaped or elongated heads, although in a few species they form small clusters of two to six or can even be solitary. They are

whitish, pink or red in colour, or shades of yellow. Each tiny flower is surrounded at the base by a tubular, five-toothed calyx of fused sepals.

The five petals are arranged like a miniature pea flower. The largest, uppermost petal is semi-erect, and is called the standard or flag petal. Two other petals form a lateral pair of wings while the basal pair form a boat-shaped keel. The petals enclose a bundle of male stamens and a long

female style with the pollen-receptive stigma at its tip. The wings and keel form a platform on which bees or other pollinating insects land. The petals turn brown after pollination, but they and the calyx persist around the ripening seed pod, which is known as a legume. The fruit splits lengthways along two seams when mature.

Farmer's friend

Clovers and other leguminous plants are good for the soil, and have traditionally been grown for fodder. Bacteria living in nodules in their roots attracts nitrogen. This enriches the soil and provides nutrition for animals. At one time farmers maintained old, clover-rich grassland and grew several species as field crops. Today only red and white clover are sown on any scale.

Some of the annual species are found mainly in southern England and near coasts. Several are plants of the Mediterranean region and southern and central Europe that have reached the north-western limit of their range in the British Isles.

White clover has creeping, self-rooting stems that enable it to spread easily. It can be a troublesome plant to eradicate once established.

Long-headed (the red subspecies *molinerii*), upright, twin-headed and starry clovers are listed in the *Red Data Book* of Britain's rarest plants. They are protected from uprooting or picking by the Wildlife and Countryside Act, 1981.

CLOVER FACT FILE

● **Bird's-foot clover or fenugreek**
Trifolium ornithopodioides
Habitat and distribution
Dry, bare or trampled sandy or gravelly places, mainly on coast; north to the Wirral and the Isle of Man, and in south and east Ireland
Size Stems prostrate, up to 20cm (8in) long
Key features
Hairless annual; leaflets blunt, toothed; 1–4 flowers 6–8mm (¼–⅜in) long, white or pale pink; seed pod longer than the calyx
Flowering time
May–August

● **Burrowing or subterranean clover**
Trifolium subterraneum
Habitat and distribution
Bare ground or short turf on sandy or gravelly soils, especially near the sea in southern Britain; one site in Co. Wicklow, Ireland
Size Stems prostrate, up to 30cm (12in) long
Key features
Hairy annual; leaflets heart-shaped, dark-spotted; 2–5 flowers (plus green sterile flowers) 8–14mm (⅜–⅝in) long, whitish to pale pink; heads of fruit pressed into the soil
Flowering time
May–July

● **White or Dutch clover**
Trifolium repens
Habitat and distribution
Common on grassy places and lawns, also sown for fodder
Size Up to 50cm (20in) tall, often smaller
Key features
Creeping, hairless perennial; leaves long-stalked, leaflets broad, toothed, usually with a whitish chevron; flowers 8–12mm (⅜–½in) long, white, richly scented, in long-stalked, spherical heads 15–25mm (⅝–1in) across; calyx with narrowly spear-shaped teeth, the two uppermost longer
Flowering time
May–November

● **Alsike clover**
Trifolium hybridum
Habitat and distribution
Grassy places, roadsides and waste ground, often as a relic of a fodder crop
Size Up to about 40cm (16in) tall
Key features
Similar to white clover but more erect, often quite robust, the leaves unmarked; flowers 7–10mm (¼–⅜in) long, white, becoming pinkish after pollination; in shorter-stalked 24–26mm (1in) heads; calyx with narrowly spear-shaped teeth of equal length
Flowering time
June–September

● **Western clover**
Trifolium occidentale
Similar to white clover but smaller – 20cm (8in) tall at most; has white or pale pink flowers May–November or even all year. A rare coastal plant in the far south-west of England, south-east Ireland and south Wales

Bird's-foot clover or fenugreek
Trifolium ornithopodioides

Burrowing or subterranean clover
Trifolium subterraneum

White or Dutch clover
Trifolium repens

Alsike clover
Trifolium hybridum

Western clover is self-pollinating, so does not rely on seasonal insects. It is therefore able to flower all year. It often grows near cultivated land and beside paths.

CLOVER FACT FILE

● Red clover
Trifolium pratense
Habitat and distribution
Common on grassy places, also sown as a fodder crop
Size Up to 60cm (2ft) tall or more, often less
Key features
Somewhat hairy perennial; leaflets oval, often with a white chevron; flowers 12–15mm (½–⅝in) long, pink or purplish pink (rarely white), in solitary or paired dense, almost stalkless egg-shaped heads 20–40mm (¾–1½in) long; calyx downy; pods egg-shaped
Flowering time
May—November

● Zigzag clover
Trifolium medium
Habitat and distribution
Widespread but local in dry grassy or scrubby places, especially on clay soils
Size Up to 50cm (20in) tall
Key features
Similar to red clover but leaflets narrower and darker green; flowers 12–15mm (½–⅝in) long and darker purplish red, in stalked, rather flat-topped heads 25–35mm (1–1⅜in) long; calyx usually hairless
Flowering time
June–August

● Sulphur clover
Trifolium ochroleucon
Habitat and distribution
Locally common in grassy places and on roadsides in east England, especially on clay soils
Size Up to 50cm (20in) tall
Key features
Perennial, like a yellow-flowered version of red clover, but leaflets narrower and unmarked; sulphur-yellow flowers 15–20mm (⅝–¾in) long, in smaller heads; the only large clover with yellow flowers
Flowering time
June–early August

● Strawberry clover
Trifolium fragiferum
Habitat and distribution
Damp, grassy places, roadsides, coastal and estuarine meadows, especially on clay soils, mainly in southern Britain
Size Up to 30cm (12in) tall
Key features
Sprawling perennial; leaves long-stalked; flowers 6–7mm (¼in) long, purplish pink, in long-stalked, almost spherical heads 10–20mm (⅜–¾in) across; calyx inflated when in fruit, producing a dull pinkish, strawberry-like head
Flowering time
June–September

● Crimson clover
Trifolium incarnatum subsp. *incarnatum*
Robust, erect annual up to 50cm (20in) tall with tapering flower heads from May to July. A scarce relic of cultivation as a fodder crop

● Long-headed clover
Trifolium incarnatum subsp. *molinerii*
Similar to crimson clover but smaller – up to 25cm (10in) tall, often less – and more tufted, with pale yellowish, sometimes pale pink, flowers in June and July. A rare plant of cliffs and rocks in west Cornwall

● Reversed clover
Trifolium resupinatum
Rare former fodder crop of southern England and Wales with purplish pink flowers

Sulphur clover
Trifolium ochroleucon

Red clover
Trifolium pratense

Strawberry clover
Trifolium fragiferum

Long-headed clover is found only on the Lizard peninsula in south-west Cornwall.

Zigzag clover
Trifolium medium

Crimson clover
Trifolium incarnatum subsp. *incarnatum*

CLOVER FACT FILE

● **Hop trefoil**
Trifolium campestre
Habitat and distribution
Dry, grassy places, usually on lime-rich soils
Size Up to 30cm (12in) tall or more
Key features
Downy annual; leaflets notched, middle one with longest stalk; flowers 4–7mm (⅙–¼in) long, pale yellow, 20–30 held in dense spherical heads 10–15mm (⅜–⅝in) across; pods covered by pale brown dead flowers
Flowering time
May–September

● **Large trefoil or large hop trefoil**
Trifolium aureum
Habitat and distribution
Introduced in grassy places
Size Up to 30cm (12in) tall or more
Key features
Similar to hop trefoil but leaflets almost stalkless; flowers 6–7mm (¼in) long, golden-yellow, in dense spherical heads 12–18mm (½–¾in) across
Flowering time
July–August

● **Lesser trefoil or suckling clover**
Trifolium dubium
Habitat and distribution
Dry, grassy places, sunny banks, lawns and bare ground including rocky areas
Size Up to 25cm (10in) tall or more
Key features
Hairy annual; middle leaflet stalked; flowers 3–4mm (⅛in) long, yellow, 10–20 held in each spherical head 5–9mm (¼–⅜in) across; egg-shaped pods covered by dead flowers
Flowering time
May–October

● **Slender trefoil**
Trifolium micranthum
Habitat and distribution
Dry, grassy places, especially shorter grass and lawns, north to Galloway; coasts only in Ireland
Size Stems often prostrate, up to 15cm (6in) long
Key features
Almost hairless annual; leaflets small, toothed; 2–6 flowers on a thread-like stalk, 2–3mm (⅛in) long, deep yellow in loose heads 4mm (⅛in) across; pods smaller than those of lesser trefoil
Flowering time
May–August

● **Clustered clover**
Trifolium glomeratum
Habitat and distribution
Rather scarce in dry, grassy or bare places, near the sea, from Norfolk to Cornwall and extreme south-east of Ireland
Size Up to 25cm (10in) tall
Key features
Hairless prostrate annual; leaves long-stalked, the leaflets short-stalked, toothed; flowers 4–5mm (⅙–¼in) long, purple-pink, in stalkless, domed heads 8–12mm (⅜–½in) across; calyx teeth pointed, curved back in fruit, like stars
Flowering time
May–July

● **Rough clover or soft trefoil**
Trifolium scabrum
Habitat and distribution
Scattered in dry, grassy and rocky places, especially by the sea, in southern Scotland; coast of east Ireland
Size Stems usually prostrate, up to 20cm (8in) long
Key features
Branched annual; leaflets downy on both sides, with veins curved backwards at the margin; flowers 4–7mm (⅙–¼in) long, white or pale pink, in stalkless, egg-shaped heads 5–12mm (¼–½in) long; calyx teeth stiff and curved backwards in fruit
Flowering time
May–July

● **Knotted clover**
Trifolium striatum
Habitat and distribution
Dry grassy or bare places, widespread but local; south coasts of Ireland often with rough clover
Size Stems spreading, up to 30cm (12in) long or more
Key features
Annual; leaflets downy on both sides, with veins straight; flowers 4–7mm (⅙–¼in) long, pink, in short, stalkless cylindrical heads 10–15mm (⅜–⅝in) long; calyx egg-shaped, ribbed, with slender, erect reddish teeth in fruit
Flowering time
Late May–July

WILDLIFE WATCH

Where do clovers grow?

- Old meadows and pastures are the best sites. Grassy roadsides and embankments are also good places to look.
- The scarcer annual clovers occur on heaths and in drier, sparse grasslands, especially near the sea on shingle beaches, cliffs, coastal paths and even gravel car parks. The smaller clovers are best searched for on hands and knees, but remember that wild plants, including clovers, should never be uprooted or damaged.

Hop trefoil
Trifolium campestre

Large trefoil or large hop trefoil
Trifolium aureum

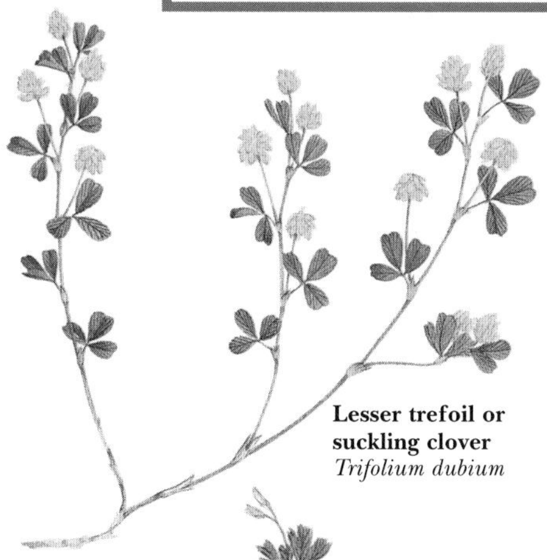
Lesser trefoil or suckling clover
Trifolium dubium

Clustered clover
Trifolium glomeratum

Slender trefoil
Trifolium micranthum

Knotted clover
Trifolium striatum

Rough clover or soft trefoil
Trifolium scabrum

CLOVER FACT FILE

● **Hare's-foot clover**
Trifolium arvense
Habitat and distribution
Dry, grassy or bare, often sandy places; scarce but coastal in Ireland
Size Up to 25cm (10in) tall
Key features
Softly haired annual or biennial; leaflets narrow, often reddish; flowers 3–6mm (⅛–¼in) long, white or pink in narrow cylindrical heads 15–25mm (⅝–1in) long; calyx teeth bristle-like in fruit
Flowering time
June–August

● **Suffocated clover**
Trifolium suffocatum
Habitat and distribution
Dry, bare or sparsely grassy places in southern England, mainly near the sea
Size Prostrate stems up to 8cm (3in) long
Key features
Hairless annual; leaflets notched, sharply toothed, held above the flowers in long-stalked rosettes; tiny flowers 2–4mm (⅛in) long, whitish, in stalkless, spherical heads 5–6mm (¼in) across; calyx teeth are pointed and curved back, almost hiding the flowers
Flowering time
March–June and
August–September

● **Sea clover**
Trifolium squamosum
Habitat and distribution
Damp, grassy places on southern coasts
Size Up to 40cm (16in) tall
Key features
Hairy annual; leaflets narrow; flowers 7–9mm (¼–⅜in) long, pale pink, in short-stalked, egg-shaped heads 10–20mm (⅜–¾in) long; calyx bell-shaped, with spreading, spine-like teeth that give fruits a star-like appearance
Flowering time
April–July

● **Upright clover**
Trifolium strictum
Habitat and distribution
Rare in dry, coastal grassland in west Cornwall, and one site on the Welsh border
Size Up to 15cm (6in) tall, often smaller
Key features
Erect hairless annual; leaflets narrow, with small, sharp glandular teeth, strongly veined and broad, whitish scale-like stipules at base; flowers 5–6mm (¼in) long, purplish pink, in dense, long-stalked, spherical heads 7–10mm (¼–⅜in) across; calyx ribbed, with long, narrow teeth
Flowering time
May–July

● **Twin-headed clover**
Trifolium bocconei
Habitat and distribution
Rare in dry, rocky grassland in west Cornwall
Size Up to 15cm (6in) tall, but often smaller
Key features
Annual; leaflets rather narrow, finely toothed; flowers 5mm (¼in) long, pale pinkish, in stalkless conical heads 9–15mm (⅜–⅝in) long, usually in unequal pairs; calyx teeth slender, hairy
Flowering time
June–July

● **Starry clover**
Trifolium stellatum
Softly haired annual, up to 20cm (8in) tall, with reddish, star-shaped fruit. Its long, pink or whitish flowers appear from May to July. A rare coastal plant found only in Sussex

Starry clover is a Mediterranean species that has become established on Shoreham beach in Sussex.

Upright clover
Trifolium strictum

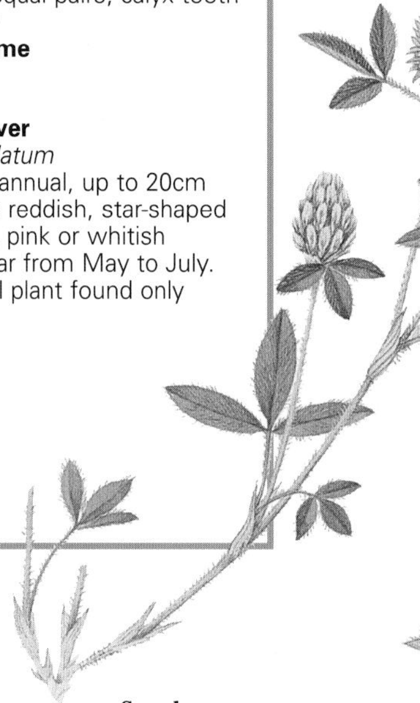

Hare's-foot clover
Trifolium arvense

Sea clover
Trifolium squamosum

Suffocated clover
Trifolium suffocatum

Twin-headed clover
Trifolium bocconei

Woodland watch

- The roe deer
- The common dormouse
- The redstart
- The bullfinch
- Recognising small warblers
- The purple emperor
- The stag beetle
- Blood-red ants
- Recognising smaller deciduous trees
- Forget-me-nots
- Climbers and scramblers

The roe deer

The shy roe deer prefers to graze near woodland thickets, but sometimes steals into suburban gardens to feed under cover of darkness. It is easiest to spot in summer when its coat turns bright russet brown.

While red deer and fallow deer may be readily seen in deer parks, roe deer are not normally kept in captivity. Territorial in their behaviour, they are less placid in temperament than other deer and are most likely to be seen alone, or in a family group of a female, called a doe, with one or two young, or kids. Living in more areas of Britain than either red or fallow deer, roe deer inhabit woods and forests throughout Scotland, northern England and the Midlands and are also spreading across southern England.

Distinguishing characteristics

The roe deer is smaller than the red or fallow deer, standing around 63–67cm (24–27in) tall at the shoulder. In summer it can be easily recognised by its bright reddish brown coat, which moults to a darker greyish brown in winter. No other British deer displays such a contrast between its summer and winter coats. In northern Britain, roe deer are often very dark in colour and some individuals may be blackish in winter.

In winter, the coat hairs, which are stiff and bristly, grow to about 55mm (2¼in) long, 50 per cent longer than they are in summer. This somewhat shaggier coat makes the roe deer look stockier and shorter-legged than in summer. Roe deer moult from around Easter onwards, looking scruffier during this time. By June, however, they have grown their rufous summer coat.

Its fairly short face gives the roe deer a neat and alert appearance, and it has a distinctive black, pointed muzzle with

In summer, the male is in peak condition, ready for mating, coat sleek and short-pronged antlers hardened. The antlers are roughened near the base and may be bloodstained where they have been rubbed against trees and shrubs.

a contrasting bright white chin. Another identifying characteristic is its rump, which the deer displays when it takes fright and runs for cover. The roe deer is easily alarmed. Unlike fallow deer, there is no black on the roe deer's tail. In fact, it is quite difficult to perceive any tail at all as it is very short – only about 5cm (2in) in length – and white so that it blends in with the patch of pale fur that surrounds it. In addition to this, the female has a tuft of long pale fur hanging from the rump.

ROE DEER FACT FILE

The roe is a medium-sized deer found across England and Scotland. Its large ears are furry inside, and it has a characteristic white chin beneath a black nose and black 'moustache' marking.

● **NAMES**
Common name: roe deer
Scientific name: *Capreolus capreolus*

● **HABITAT**
Mainly woodland, including young plantations with plenty of undergrowth; open moorland in Scotland; reedy marshland and occasionally farmland; some suburban areas

● **DISTRIBUTION**
Throughout Scotland, northern England and the Midlands; scattered in the south; absent from Ireland, Isle of Man and Isle of Wight and Wales

● **STATUS**
Around 300,000 individuals in Britain with numbers increasing

● **SIZE**
Height 63–67cm (24½–27in) at the shoulder, head and neck another 30cm (12in); weight adult 18–30kg (39½–66lb); bucks slightly bigger and heavier than does

● **KEY FEATURES**
Coat sandy to reddish brown in summer, greyish brown to blackish in winter; tail inconspicuous, variable pale buff rump patch; black nose and nose band, white chin; short antlers with maximum of three points

● **HABITS**
Normally solitary or in small family groups; mostly nocturnal but often seen out in the daytime browsing for food

● **VOICE**
Sharp, dog-like bark; occasional squeals when alarmed

● **FOOD**
Shrubs and young trees, including foliage, bark, fruit and nuts, and especially acorns; also feeds on vegetation from a wide range of plants such as grasses, ferns, heathers and brambles; woodland fungi

● **BREEDING**
Rut from July to late August, and kids born in the following year from May to June; single kid or twins, occasionally triplets

● **YOUNG**
Brown with white spots; resemble adults within a few months

● **SIGNS**
Greenish black oval droppings, usually found in small clusters

The male's antlers are cast in November or December. New ones grow over the winter, protected from frost and damage by a furry sheath.

Distribution map key

■ Present

□ Not present

Ears are large and furry inside.

Sleek, foxy red summer coat darkens to greyish brown in winter.

White chin patch contrasts with a black nose and 'moustache'.

A long tuft of hairs, known as the anal tush, hangs from the female's rump.

Strong but slender legs give the roe deer its leaping ability.

Crown of spikes

The male roe deer – called a 'buck', not a stag – carries short, spiky antlers, which do not grow beyond about 25cm (10in) at most. In common with all deer, the female has no antlers. Unlike other deer, the buck's antlers have a rough, knobbly surface to their main stem, which looks as if it is thickly encrusted with brown cement. The prongs, or tines, that branch off from this are smooth and there are normally only two or three on each antler.

Bucks have a well-developed coronet, which is a thickened ring where the antler rises from a bony stalk on the skull. This stalk, called a pedicle, may be visible when the kid is just four months old. Sometimes the pedicle has little bony buttons, but these often fall off after three to five months.

The male grows a first set of antlers, which form a single short spike, at about nine months old. Each new set is larger than the previous one until, after about two years, the antlers reach their maximum size. The size of the antlers, and their number of points, is not a reliable guide to the age of roe deer because their antlers are never very large, tending to become thick rather than long. Thick antlers indicate that the deer are roaming in an area with plentiful food rather than being a sign of old age. However, the thickest antlers are likely to belong to deer more than three years old.

Antlers are shed during the winter and regrown in the following weeks. The new antlers form inside a protective covering of woolly skin, referred to as velvet, that is shed around April time. Bucks often thrash their heads against trees or shrubs to assist in freeing the antlers from their

furry sheaths, and in doing so, spread scent from their facial glands. This sends a territorial signal to other deer in the neighbourhood.

Curiously, some bucks fail to rid themselves of the velvet, or to cast their antlers, and the coverings remain, thickening with each passing year. This may be due to low levels of the male hormone testosterone in the blood. Bucks that keep their velvet are referred to as having a 'perruque' head. (Perruque is French for 'wig'.)

In winter, the roe deer's coat becomes dark greyish brown, making the pale rump patch stand out. When the deer is alarmed, the hairs of the rump patch become erect so that the pale patch of fur resembles a large powder puff.

Long history

Roe deer have lived in Britain for centuries. During the harshest periods of the Ice Age there would have been few forests to provide them with food, but as the climate improved, they roamed across from the Continent,

Fleeing fast

A roe deer may be tempted into the open in daylight by its favourite food – brambles, for instance, growing in a woodland clearing. If disturbed when browsing, though, the deer will immediately take flight.

Long slender limbs allow the deer to make a quick getaway. The doe runs swiftly and gracefully, interspersing its fluid gait with graceful leaps. Exceptionally agile, it can, if necessary, clear fences and other obstacles in one spectacular leap.

to which Britain was linked until about 9000 years ago. As trees became more abundant, so the roe deer moved to new areas, but as the forests grew thicker, they became less suitable for roe deer, and over succeeding centuries, fewer and fewer survived until they remained in just a few remote areas.

The current population is mainly the result of reintroductions from Europe during the past 200 years, because they were in demand for hunting. Roe deer were released in Dorset in 1800, for example, and in the 1880s a number were imported from Germany into East Anglia. More were released in the Lake District to supplement numbers there. Now, with more woodland being preserved, or planted, around Britain, roe deer are

▲ At about two years old, a buck claims a territory that it will occupy until ousted by a younger male. In late May, when the antlers are hard and fully grown, the buck rubs the glands on its head against trees and shrubs to leave scent to warn off rivals.

◀ When snow covers the ground, roe deer must use their hooves and muzzles to scrape through the frosty blanket to feed on the grasses, fungi, ivy and ferns that are hidden below.

roaming more widely than ever and spreading rapidly to new areas. Recent observations suggest they may soon reach Wales.

Forest cover

Roe deer normally live in woodland, but they sometimes wander on to open moors, even those high in the mountains of Scotland. They will live on farmland and raid crops, but usually only where there are nearby forests and thickets to which they can run for cover. Roe deer thrive in young forestry plantations at the stage just before the trees form a dense thicket and are thinned out. In such conditions, the deer population may increase so that there are more than 20 per square kilometre (52 per square mile).

As the trees grow they cast an increasingly dense shadow, throwing the shrubs and grasses on which the deer feed into deep shade where they cannot flourish. As a result, older forests do not provide enough food for the high numbers of deer that a young plantation can support. This is particularly true of conifer plantations where, as the trees get taller, the lower branches die back, so that the nourishing parts grow out of reach of deer. Typically, the number of deer living in such plantations halves by the time the trees are about 20 years old.

As well as eating the leaves and gnawing the bark of young trees, roe deer tend to thrash the branches around, both in their search for food and in their efforts to

The deer's bounding strides serve to emphasise the white rump patch, which bobs up and down. This acts as an eye-catching signal of potential danger to other deer.

On the alert

Without the security provided by the many ears, eyes and noses of a herd, roe deer are always wary. They have acute senses of smell and hearing. This doe constantly swivels her large, sensitive ears in order to detect anything remotely unusual.

Roe deer have excellent vision for spotting moving objects, but they have difficulty seeing objects that remain motionless because they see virtually no colour.

shed their antler velvet. As a result, many trees become misshapen and fail to grow properly. In managed woodland, foresters are generally keen to keep numbers of deer in check, which they do by culling, in order to limit the amount of tree damage.

Typically, roe deer feed about nine times in the course of 24 hours. They are ruminants and so, after eating, they rest and regurgitate their food, chewing it thoroughly again. After that, the food passes through several stomach chambers to the gut. Roe deer often feed in the half light of dawn and dusk, but their behaviour is influenced by disturbance. Where there is a lot of human activity, the deer are likely to be largely nocturnal and spend the day hidden in dense cover.

Defending territory

During winter, roe deer may live together in small groups, but they never form large herds. In summer, the bucks mostly live alone, fending off intruders. The does may stay in a small family group with their young from the previous year. In general, bucks are territorial from about Easter until late summer, but not all the males hold territories. Those that do not probably do not breed either. Bucks with territories bark aggressively and chase other deer away. They also mark trees and shrubs with scent to warn off trespassing rivals. It is rare for fights to occur, however.

A territory in good feeding areas may be as small as 7 hectares (17 acres). In the north, territories may be four or five times larger, especially on open moorland. Territories often remain the same, defended by one buck and inherited by another. In winter, bucks roam much more widely.

Does tend to stay on familiar home ground. When a doe dies, its area is taken over by a younger female, usually a daughter. The home ranges of does often overlap with each other and with the larger territories of one or more bucks.

▲ Roe deer sometimes raid gardens in daylight, although they do so more often at night. Cloven hoof prints in flowerbeds are a sign of their visit.

FEEDING HABITS

Roe deer prefer to feed by plucking leaves and shoots from deciduous trees, especially young saplings. In conifer woods they eat the growing tips of tree branches. They also feed on shrubs, such as brambles and wild roses. In winter, when there are fewer green leaves to eat, the deer turn to other foods such as fungi, ivy and ferns. During the rest of the year they may favour seasonal vegetation, such as acorns in the autumn or soft young holly leaves in early summer. Roe deer are adept at seeking out the most nutritious parts of the plants. They do not normally consume large amounts of low-grade food such as hay or dead leaves.

In recent years, the spread of roe deer into the fringes of towns – even into the outskirts of London – has been encouraged by the range of nutritious plants unintentionally provided for them by urban gardeners. The presence of deer is not always welcome because they eat many ornamental shrubs such as roses and fuchsias as well as other flowering plants. In only two or three visits, roe deer can clear a garden of its flowers.

▲ Roe deer are attracted to cornfields but will usually eat the wild flowers rather than the crop itself.

◄ Although they browse on tree shoots, roe deer do not stand on their hind legs to feed. Below the browse line, however, they may strip trees entirely of new buds so that the trees grow in a misshapen form.

▶ Although roe deer often give birth to a single kid, twins are more common. Does even produce triplets occasionally, especially where food is plentiful.

▼ Newborn kids are left in long grass or hidden beneath shrubs. The doe is always nearby and returns to suckle them several times a day. To reduce the risk of losing both to a predator, twins are hidden separately rather than together.

Unusual pregnancy

Roe deer mate in high summer but, uniquely among deer, the fertilised egg lies inside the female in a state of suspended development. Pregnancy does not begin until about December so that the young are not born in late winter when bad weather and little food would reduce the chance of survival. Instead, they are born from mid-May into early June when conditions are more favourable. Does often return to the same place each year to have their young. When it is time to give birth, they become solitary and aggressive towards other deer.

Raising kids

Newborn kids are covered with dark brown fur and dappled with white spots. Their eyes are open and, within hours of birth, they can follow their mother as she moves about to feed. She provides them with milk for six to eight weeks while they learn to feed themselves. They may take vegetation into their mouths when they are as young as four days old, soon discarding it again. They start to eat solid food after a week. The white spots on the kids' coats fade after about six weeks, and disappear at the first moult in the autumn. Growing steadily, the young cut their permanent teeth the following year.

They now look like adults and, continuing to mature, breed for the first time at about 14 months. Young does may be allowed to remain on the edge of their mothers' home ranges but when young bucks are a year or two old, they are usually driven away by adults of both sexes, unless a buck inherits its father's territory. This is often the case as bucks rarely hold a territory for more than about three years before being succeeded by younger males.

Many dangers threaten roe deer, even though their main natural predator – the wolf – is now extinct in Britain. Golden eagles and wild cats are also no longer a danger to kids except in some parts of Scotland. However, dogs, foxes and cars take their toll, as do parasites and disease. Kids are particularly vulnerable. More than half do not survive their first year, and nearly three-quarters die before they are old enough to breed. The average life span of roe deer is about two to three years, although some can live for 10 years or more – in rare cases up to 16 years.

Roe deer can run at impressive speed, reaching about 32km/h (20mph) at full gallop, their bodies outstretched. When threatened, a buck's flight reaction is instant.

The common dormouse

As daylight fades, a dormouse curled up in its tree nest rouses itself from its slumbers. Relying on an excellent sense of smell, this agile rodent scrambles among the branches, balancing on the thinnest twigs to reach a choice morsel.

The common dormouse may spend eight hours or more in its nest every day. Spring and summer nests are made above ground in hedgerows or trees but winter nests are normally built at ground level, often under leaf litter.

Spotting a common dormouse in the wild is never easy. Even in its active phase during the summer, the creature's nocturnal, tree-climbing habits and its general scarcity make it a rare sight indeed.

The common dormouse, which belongs to the family Gliridae, begins to come out of hibernation in April, later in the north of Britain. At first, it is awake for brief periods only but these gradually become longer until the little rodent is fully active in May, although it still sleeps during the day. It feeds on hawthorn, caterpillars and aphids, among other flowers and insects, so that it will be in peak condition for mating in late May or early June, which is late compared with other British rodents. The young are born usually in July or early August when flowers and fruit are plentiful. There are normally four, but sometimes as many as seven, young in a litter. Nests have been found containing more than eight babies and this may be the result of two females sharing the workload of raising their families.

By the autumn dormice are busy fattening up for their winter hibernation. They are especially fond of hazel nuts – an alternative name for the common dormouse is hazel dormouse – as well as beech nuts and blackberries. They will

HELPING DORMICE

Wildlife trusts manage reserves where dormice are present, and from time to time hold working parties to help regenerate derelict coppices. Volunteers are usually welcome.

Nesting boxes have proved to be very successful at helping encourage and maintain dormouse populations at known sites, so making these and donating them to reserves is of great benefit.

Searching for signs of dormice in woodlands where they are not known to occur, or where they once did occur but have not been seen recently, can help identify places that might otherwise be overlooked. Local wildlife trusts are always pleased to hear the results of such observations.

The dormouse normally raises one litter per year but in exceptionally warm years, with plenty of food, it may breed twice.

also seek out yew trees to feast on their red berries. In warm years a second brood may be born at this time, but young dormice born late in the season may not be able to find enough food to fatten up sufficiently before the first hard frosts occur. A good supply of hazel nuts and sweet chestnuts, some of the last foods to ripen in the autumn, is absolutely essential for their winter survival.

Most dormice hibernate from October but by mid-November all will be curled up in their warm nests to spend the next five months or so asleep. Hibernation is a successful survival strategy. While other small mammals struggle to find food and keep warm in the cold winter climate, the dormouse sleeps through it all, living off the body fat that it has accumulated during the autumn.

The dormouse is completely inactive during hibernation, and its metabolic rate slows to almost nothing. Its body temperature drops so low that it feels cold to the touch – it is normally only a degree or two warmer than its surroundings – and its rate of respiration slows dramatically. As long as the dormouse goes into hibernation weighing at least 12–15g (about ½oz), it should have sufficient reserves to last through a long winter.

Threats to dormice
A long, cold winter provides the ideal conditions for hibernating dormice. Curiously, problems are more likely to arise if the winter is very mild. This is because the dormouse may wake up and go in search of food that is not there, wasting valuable reserves that cannot be replenished until spring. The mild winters of south-west Britain, for example, are not conducive to long periods of hibernation, which are much more likely in the drier, colder winters typical of the south-east.

COMMON DORMOUSE FACT FILE

A rare and protected species, the common dormouse's survival depends largely on the conservation of suitable woodland where it can breed in summer and sleep undisturbed throughout the winter.

● NAMES
Common names: common dormouse, hazel dormouse
Scientific name: *Muscardinus avellanarius*

● HABITAT
Mixed deciduous woodland, copses, hedgerows where a variety of berry and seed-bearing trees and shrubs occur, especially hazel and honeysuckle; thrives in sunny, dry conditions

● DISTRIBUTION
Scattered populations in England and Wales as far north as Northumberland

● STATUS
Probably 45,000 individuals in England and Wales

● SIZE
Head and body 60–90mm (2⅜–3½in), tail length 55–70mm (2¼–2¾in), weight 15–40g (½–1½oz)

● KEY FEATURES
Bushy tail, bright orange-brown or reddish fur, large black eyes, short muzzle and long whiskers

● HABITS
Nocturnal and arboreal, emerging at night to clamber through vegetation in search of food. Returns to nest before dawn and spends eight hours in normal sleep. Hibernates for 5–6 months each year in small nest on woodland floor

● VOICE
Wheezing sounds when awakening from hibernation, occasional shrill squeaks when alarmed, and some purring or mewing sounds, but mostly silent

● FOOD
Nuts, especially hazel and beech; seeds, berries, pollen, nectar-bearing plants and insects

● BREEDING
2–7 young, usually born July–August after gestation of 3½ weeks; occasional second litter in early autumn

● NEST
Compact, tightly woven ball of shredded honeysuckle bark and leaves; in summer, sometimes built in old bird's nest or squirrel's drey; in winter, on woodland floor among leaf litter; readily uses nesting boxes

● YOUNG
Born blind and naked; fur grows at about 1 week old and is greyer than adult's

Distribution map key

■ Present

□ Not present

PROTECTED!

Under the provisions of the Wildlife and Countryside Act, 1986, it is illegal to kill or injure a common dormouse, or to disturb it in its nest.

A baby dormouse, about two weeks old, suckles from its mother. Young dormice may remain with their mother for up to two months.

An acute sense of hearing keeps the dormouse alert for the approach of predators at night.

Forward-facing eyes allow the dormouse to judge distances.

Long digits and thickened pads on the feet give a firm grip.

Dormice build their nests mainly from shredded honeysuckle bark woven into a ball, often with an outer layer of leaves.

WILDLIFE WATCH

Where can I see dormice in the wild?

● Copses that are linked to larger woodlands by a network of hedgerows and corridors of uncultivated land are excellent places to look for dormice. Very small copses and short stretches of hedgerow are not suitable because they do not contain enough food for dormice and all the other small mammals with which they compete.

● In summer, look out for cream and yellow flowers of honeysuckle scattered on the ground under hedgerows. Dormice pull the flowers off the shoots before they have been pollinated so that they can eat the sugary nectar.

● In autumn, look for nibbled hazel nut shells. Dormice eat the nuts where they find them and drop the shells to the ground.

● If work is being carried out in a wood, a dormouse may be disturbed. In this case, it will always rush upwards, climbing towards the tree canopy.

● Most wildlife trusts in southern England now have at least one reserve where dormice are a special feature. For further information contact the Mammal Society at 2B Inworth Street, London SW11 3EP (telephone 020 7350 2200) or visit www.mammal.org.uk

Owl pellets are among the best indicators of which small mammals are present in a woodland, but the remains of dormice are rarely found in them. Tawny owls do sometimes take dormice but voles and wood mice seem to be much easier prey. This may be partly because they are much more numerous. Dormice are so scarce that the chances of a predator finding them, especially when other small mammals are so abundant, are low.

Weasels sometimes take dormice, and cats occasionally catch them. However, most dormice live for two to three years –
some for as long as five or more years – and die as a result of low food reserves, bad weather or disease rather than being eaten by a predator.

Home territory

Dormice are well adapted for life in trees. Their long tails aid balance when running along branches or when sitting on a twig. The ideal dormouse habitat contains a

The name dormouse probably derives from the Latin 'dormire', which means to sleep – an appropriate name for a creature that spends most of its time in hibernation.

mixture of native trees and shrubs, providing a succession of fruits, seeds, nuts and berries throughout the late spring, summer and early autumn. Dense thickets of bramble and curtains of twining honeysuckle provide cover for nesting as well as additional food supplies. An interlocking growth of stems and branches enables the dormouse to clamber around in search of food without ever coming down to ground level. All it needs for nesting and survival can be found among the branches.

Curiously, pigs and dormice do not mix. Woodlands such as the New Forest that have a long tradition of 'pannage' – free-range pigs foraging in the winter – now have few or none of the little mammals. The reason for the conflict is thought to be the result of the way pigs root around for acorns on the woodland floor. In the process they may disturb, crush or even eat hibernating dormice.

◀ The dormouse makes the best use of whatever food is available, including berries in late summer and autumn. It has a varied diet and cannot survive on just leaves and grasses.

▼ Discarded hazel-nut shells provide a clue to the presence of dormice. They have a unique way of opening hazel nuts, making a neat round hole with a smooth, bevelled edge to the opening. Search for them beneath the outermost branches of fruiting hazel trees and use a hand lens to check on the tooth marks. Wood mice and bank voles make toothmarks that leave a rough edge to the hole and squirrels always crack the nuts apart.

The redstart

This brightly coloured summer visitor nests in open woodland, seeking out nooks and crevices in the oaks, beeches or pines. With red tail constantly quivering, either parent fetches insects, caterpillars and spiders for the hungry brood.

One of Britain's most handsome visitors is the redstart. The male has a bluish grey crown and back, and reddish underparts. A white forehead separates the black face and throat from a blue-grey crown. By contrast, the female has predominantly brown and orangey buff plumage. All the birds have a bright orange-red rump and tail.

A member of the chat group of the thrush family, the redstart has a shy, timid nature. Often only its red tail is glimpsed as the bird dashes for the cover of a hidden perch. Part of its name is derived from '*steort*' – the Anglo-Saxon for 'tail'. For the redstart, the tail is especially important because the bird uses it to draw attention to itself. For example, the male flashes his tail to attract a mate and guide the female to a chosen nest site.

Woodland arrivals

Redstarts arrive in Britain from central Africa in mid-April and May, and leave from late August to September. They live in varied woodland, from the tall, dense oak and beech woods of the New Forest to the ancient Caledonian pine woods of Scotland. In the oak woodland that cloaks the steep hillsides of Wales, there can be more than 60 pairs per square kilometre (155 per square mile). Other favoured places include alongside wooded streams and rivers, on open, bushy, upland hillsides, and in parks and gardens.

Most male redstarts arrive in Britain under cover of darkness during the latter half of April. For the first few days after their arrival at a suitable place, the birds are quite quiet, spending all their waking hours feeding. After their long migration, they need to rebuild their strength. During this time, a male will even tolerate other males in a future territory.

Once restored to peak condition, the males begin to sing and establish territories in preparation for the arrival of the females a few days later. At first, a territory may be larger than necessary but, as more males arrive, it shrinks until a compromise size has been reached – this

A male redstart brings insect food for its brood, which is concealed in a well-hidden nest located in a cranny among the roots of an upturned tree.

REDSTART FACT FILE

Shy and skulking by nature, the redstart feeds mainly in the trees, but also ventures warily down to the woodland floor where it hops, robin-like, probing the leaf litter for insects and worms. In flight, it often makes sudden turns in order to take cover.

● **NAMES**
Common names: redstart, common redstart
Scientific name: *Phoenicurus phoenicurus*

● **HABITAT**
Woodland, especially sessile oak and open pine woods, parkland, orchards and gardens

● **DISTRIBUTION**
Much of southern, western and northern England; most of Wales and Scotland, except north east; a few pairs scattered in Ireland

● **STATUS**
Around 90,000 pairs breed but population flunctuates considerably and in good years there may be as many as 300,000

● **SIZE**
Length 14cm (5½in); wingspan 20–24cm (8–9½in); weight 14–18g (½–¾oz)

● **KEY FEATURES**
Breeding male has bluish grey back, white forehead, black face and throat, orange-red breast and flanks; females brownish grey above, buff-white below; rufous tail

● **HABITS**
Active morning and evening; may hover when feeding on insects on foliage

● **VOICE**
Male sings short, rather melancholy warble, usually introduced by a '*hwee*' note often combined with '*tic*' notes, '*hwee-tic-tic-tic*'

● **FOOD**
Flying insects, caterpillars, worms and spiders; also berries in autumn

● **BREEDING**
Late April–August; often two broods

● **NEST**
A loose cup of grass, moss and other vegetation, lined with feathers and animal hair

● **EGGS**
5–7 glossy, pale blue eggs; incubated by female for 13–14 days

● **YOUNG**
Brown and speckly; fledge in 14–16 days

The female has duller, more camouflaged plumage than the male, in keeping with her role as nest maker and carer for the brood. However, she too has a bright, orange-red rump and tail, which distinguishes her from most other small brown birds.

Breeding male has black mask and throat.

Back is a bluish grey.

Underparts are bright reddish orange.

Distribution map key

■ Present during breeding season

■ Spring and autumn passage migrant

□ Not present

---

is large enough to provide sufficient food for a redstart family, yet small enough for one male to defend.

Attracting a mate

The males' strength and vigour, along with the brightness of their plumage, enable them not only to defend territories but to attract a mate. When the females arrive, the males court them. Each male encourages any female that passes to remain in his territory. Once a female has accepted the advances of a particular male and settled in a territory, the male performs a greeting ceremony. Landing on a branch just in front of the female, the male crouches with tail fanned and wings spread. Beak raised and wide open, he gives a high-pitched hissing call.

If the call sufficiently impresses the desired mate, the male lures the female to a chosen nest site using a number of display tactics. These include clinging to the nest site, just below the entrance hole, with tail fanned. The male may also perch inside, head poking out, to sing a song. Occasionally, the male performs a gliding song flight, heading for the nest site with wings and tail spread.

Depending on her condition and the availability of food, the female begins to build a nest about a week after arriving.

Redstarts commonly nest in dry-stone walls and holes in trees, but they take readily to nestboxes. Once the male has chosen a site, flying rapidly in and out of the entrance is one way to attract the female's attention.

REDSTART CALENDAR

MARCH • APRIL

By March, redstarts have left Africa and are flying over southern Europe. Males precede the females by a few days and, in mid-April, reach British woods and claim territories with song.

MAY • JUNE

In May, males begin courting females and encouraging them to build nests. From mid-May, the brown, speckled young hatch and demand a constant supply of food.

JULY • AUGUST

By early August, the young have fledged – the juveniles stay together for up to three weeks before dispersing. Adult birds become especially secretive as they prepare to moult for migration.

SEPTEMBER • FEBRUARY

In October, plumage now duller, the last redstarts leave Britain's shores and head south. Continental birds may be blown on to the east coast of Britain during their autumn migration.

With hungry nestlings to feed, this male redstart is kept busy, bringing beakfuls of caterpillars and spiders back to his mate. The young remain in the nest for about two weeks.

The female builds the nest without the help of the male. Unless interrupted by bad weather, she may well complete the nest in about five days. The male remains quiet during this time so that he does not attract the attention of predators, such as cats and magpies, to the nest. Once egg laying starts, the male resumes full song. The female produces five to seven glossy, pale blue eggs and begins incubating them after laying the final egg.

Hungry mouths

When the young hatch, about two weeks after the last egg is laid, the male brings them small insects, caterpillars and spiders. The female may share the food among the nestlings, but usually the male feeds them for the first five or six days. The female broods them to keep them warm, but soon also goes out in search of food to satisfy their growing appetites.

Catching insects

Redstarts, especially males, are adept at taking insects on the wing in brief forays from open perches. They also catch them on the woodland floor, scrutinising the ground below before darting down to snatch them up. While hopping on the woodland floor, redstarts may pick up insects from the leaf litter.

Moving forwards, the bird adopts an aggressive stance, with neck extended, plumage sleeked down and tail fanned.

A male redstart, hunting for food to feed its young, spots an insect such as a mayfly instantly.

Watching intently, the male prepares to dart after the insect and catch it in flight.

BLACK REDSTART

The black redstart can be distinguished from the common redstart by its darker plumage. In spring, the male takes on breeding colours of a dusky slate-grey head and back, and sooty black face, chin and upper breast, fading to grey on the belly. It often quivers its rufous or orange-red tail. The female is mainly dusky greyish brown with the same reddish tail.

Male black redstarts often perch on television aerials and rooftops to sing. Their song resembles that of the redstart,

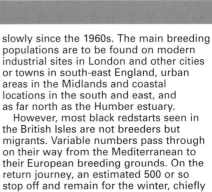

but is shorter and perhaps sweeter. It has a major distinguishing feature, however. During the repeated song phrases, the males include a peculiar sound that has been likened to ball bearings rattling, two sheets of coarse sandpaper being rubbed together or scrunching gravel. This part of the song is brief but distinctive.

After the Second World War, black redstarts started nesting in bombed areas, where the rubble was similar to the rock scree and boulder-strewn hills of their homes on mainland Europe, where they are abundant. Only around 80–120 pairs of black redstarts breed each year in Britain, although numbers have been increasing

slowly since the 1960s. The main breeding populations are to be found on modern industrial sites in London and other cities or towns in south-east England, urban areas in the Midlands and coastal locations in the south and east, and as far north as the Humber estuary.

However, most black redstarts seen in the British Isles are not breeders but migrants. Variable numbers pass through on their way from the Mediterranean to their European breeding grounds. On the return journey, an estimated 500 or so stop off and remain for the winter, chiefly around the south and west coasts.

◄ **The male black redstart is predominantly dusky black with a striking chestnut rump and tail and white wing bar. It is less shy than the redstart and more likely to be seen running quickly along the ground.**

► **Breeding begins in late April, when the female often chooses a ledge or crevice in an old building or factory to build her nest. The four to six fluffy, grey young fledge after about two weeks.**

After about two weeks, the speckled young are ready to leave the nest, which they do one by one over a period of a few hours. They usually stay together as a family group, which makes it easier for their parents to locate them and provide them with food. The adults continue to do this for another two to three weeks, until the young become independent.

Warning calls

If danger threatens, the adults give their characteristic 'hwee' alarm call, which is usually followed by one to three 'tic' calls. The latter distinguishes redstarts from nightingales, chaffinches and willow warblers, which have similar calls to signal the approach of a predator. It is possible that a shared alarm note is mutually beneficial to these small woodland birds.

Autumn migration

During July and the first half of August, redstarts moult in preparation for their autumn migration. Feathers grown the previous year are now worn and tatty, and unsuitable for the long journey ahead. Juveniles moult just their head and body feathers, but the adults undergo a full and protracted moult. A little incapacitated by this, redstarts become even more wary to avoid detection by predators.

From mid-August onwards, redstarts begin the long journey back to their African winter quarters. Many pause in

Insects, such as caterpillars, are usually gleaned from the foliage of trees and other vegetation. Redstarts hunt at all levels of the woodland, from the tree tops to the leaf litter on the ground.

southern France to regain their strength before crossing the Pyrenees and Spain. They rest once more at the southern end of the Iberian Peninsula, before traversing northern Africa and the Sahara, probably in a single flight.

In spring, when redstarts return to their favourite, mainly woodland, haunts in Britain, they make a more leisurely journey. Most of the redstart's migratory flights are undertaken at night – guided by the moon and stars.

WILDLIFE WATCH

Where can I see redstarts?

● Look in oak woodlands in the New Forest, Dartmoor, Exmoor, the Welsh border country and mid-Wales, the Peak District and the Lake District, the Pennines and the North York Moors. The Coombes Valley RSPB Reserve in Staffordshire also supports redstarts.

● Visit other broad-leaved woodlands, such as Mark Ash Wood in the New Forest, Hampshire. However, the redstarts are often very high up in the canopy here. In May, listen for the males' song.

● Sessile oak woodlands in the hills and valleys of mid-Wales harbour redstarts, including the Dinas RSPB Reserve, Carmarthenshire, and the Elan Valley area, west of Rhayader.

● In Scotland, both broad-leaved woods and the ancient Caledonian pine forests of Speyside have many redstarts. The RSPB reserve at Loch Garten is a good place to visit.

The bullfinch

A colourful bird with a plaintive call, the bullfinch is most likely to be seen with its mate. Adult birds eat mainly seeds and buds but, in summer, both parents are kept busy hunting for insects to feed their young.

A soft, piping '*dew*' heard emanating from the depths of a thick hedgerow is most likely to be the call of a bullfinch. A glimpse of this shy bird may consist of little more than a black tail and startling white rump as it takes flight and heads for cover. Bullfinches are becoming increasingly scarce in Britain, however, and opportunities to see them, or to hear their subtle calls, are diminishing.

One of Britain's most easily recognised small birds, the male bullfinch is particularly striking. Its bright blush-pink breast, blue-grey back, and glossy black cap and tail are unmistakable. The female has the same basic plumage pattern, but with a brownish back and dull salmon-pink underparts, while the juvenile is mostly brown, except for its white rump, and has no black cap. It is not surprising that this finch was a popular cagebird in the past, and is still bred in captivity for showing at cagebird exhibitions.

Feeding habits

The bullfinch's bill is short, rounded and strong, with sharp edges. It is a tool for nipping buds, shoots and fruit, then crushing and peeling them. Unusually for finches, bullfinches often discard the soft, outer flesh of fruits to eat the seeds. This is why they can be seen feeding on brambles after the fruit has withered.

However, their diet consists mainly of softer seeds of native trees, particularly the winged seeds of the ash tree, but when these become scarce, the birds leave

▶ With a bill full of crushed berries, this male bullfinch scans its surroundings before continuing to feed. The bullfinch is around the size of a house sparrow and has a neck so thick as to be hardly noticeable.

▼ Young bullfinches grow quickly on a nutritious diet of insects, provided by both parents. The adults gather food in pouches, which are newly formed each spring in the floor of their mouths.

BULLFINCH FACT FILE

A bird of woodlands, thickets and hedges, the bullfinch is present all year in most of Britain. Its white rump is particularly noticeable in flight, which is undulating over long distances, although it seldom travels far.

● **NAMES**
Common names: bullfinch, Eurasian bullfinch
Scientific name: *Pyrrhula pyrrhula*

● **HABITAT**
Undergrowth near woodland edges, hedgerows and gardens

● **DISTRIBUTION**
Throughout most of British Isles

● **STATUS**
Around 190,000 pairs; numbers falling

● **SIZE**
Length 15cm (6in); weight 22–25g (about 1oz)

● **KEY FEATURES**
Thick neck with short, stubby bill; blue-grey back, black cap and black tail with snowy white rump; male has bright pinkish red underparts; female has a dull grey nape with black cap and greyish olive upperparts, and pinkish brown underparts; juvenile is browner and lacks a black cap

● **HABITS**
Shy, keeps mostly to dense cover; rarely seen on the ground; weak-looking flight

● **VOICE**
Mostly a short, simple, but far-carrying, low, piping *'dew'*; song a creaky warble, rarely heard

● **FOOD**
Seeds, berries, buds and shoots; a few invertebrates and small snails; young fed on plant material and insects

● **BREEDING**
May–July; 1, 2, or sometimes 3 broods

● **NEST**
Built in bushes and trees; flimsy structure of twigs, moss and lichen, lined with fine roots, animal hair and grass

● **EGGS**
3–7, usually 4–5 pale bluish eggs with dark purple-brown markings; incubated by female for 12–14 days.

● **YOUNG**
Fed by both parents; leave nest after 14–16 days; breed at 1 year old

Most bullfinches rear their first family of the season in early May, laying up to five pale greenish blue eggs. The chicks hatch over two to four days, and remain in the nest for around two weeks.

Nape and mantle are bluish grey.

Wings are black with a broad white wingbar.

The bill is black and stubby.

Male has pinkish red underparts.

Tail is black and wedge-shaped.

Rump and undertail are brilliant white.

Distribution map key

Present all year round

Present during summer months

Present during winter months

Not present

woods and hedgerows to feed in orchards and gardens. Their predilection for fruit trees and flowering shrubs in spring has made them unpopular with gardeners and especially in the commercial fruit-growing areas of southern and western England. Bullfinches can eat spring buds at the rate of 30 or so every minute.

The crop damage that bullfinches can inflict was recognised as long ago as the 16th century, when they were targeted as pests with a bounty of a penny a head established by law. In the mid-20th century, 200 birds were killed in a single Herefordshire garden each year over a period of five years, yet the local population remained stable.

There are compensations however, as bullfinches eat the seeds and buds of many plants that farmers and gardeners consider to be weeds. They also feed their young on insects and other invertebrates, many of which are regarded as pests.

Breeding pairs
Unlike most finches, the bullfinch is rarely seen in flocks. It is more usual to see a single bird or, most likely, a pair

Northern migrants look very similar to native bullfinches, except they are generally slightly larger and more brightly coloured, as in this vivid-breasted male.

Feeding in gardens

The bullfinch supplements its main diet of tree seeds in late summer and autumn with seeds and berries of shrubs. It is not averse to taking garden bird seed mixes from bird tables or pecking at the remains of flowering shrubs.

The dried seed head of a garden honeysuckle offers food to a hungry bullfinch.

The bird takes care to obtain a good grip on a seed with its stubby bill.

Pulling downwards and backwards, the bullfinch works hard to snap or break off a husk from the cluster.

It extracts the seed efficiently from the hard husk. The bullfinch feeds by carefully manipulating buds and seeds in its bill.

although a group may congregate near a winter food supply. Pair bonds are formed before the breeding season and, if both birds survive, they usually stay together through the autumn and winter. Young bullfinches and adults that have lost their mates start to form pairs in March or April and, by the beginning of May, it is unusual to see a bullfinch on its own. The male chases away potential rivals while the female builds a nest. This comprises two layers – a loose base of twigs lined with an inner cup of moss, fine roots and lichen. Once nesting, bullfinches do not defend a territory. There have been reports of two nests built in the same bush, and even of two females sharing a nest.

Successful pairs often raise two or even three broods in a season. The female incubates the eggs, but both parents feed the chicks. Although adult bullfinches eat mainly plant matter, they feed their young – at least initially – partly on insects and other invertebrates. The parent birds have a special adaptation to help them collect food for their young during the breeding season. They develop pouches in the floor of their mouths, underneath their tongues, in which they can store food. The two sacs – one on either side of the tongue – hold a surprising amount of food. It has been estimated that the pouch's capacity is up to one square centimetre, which is enough to hold a lot of small insects or seeds.

Foreign migrants

British bullfinches seldom travel far, and there are few records of birds crossing to Europe. However, a few migrants from the Continent appear on British east coasts and the Northern Isles of Scotland. Bullfinches from Scandinavia often arrive on the tiny island of Fair Isle, between

▲ Bird seed mixtures make easy pickings for a bullfinch. Unusually among finches, these birds sometimes also eat small snails, crushing them in their strong bills.

▶ Spraying droplets in all directions, the bird ruffles its feathers exuberantly in the shallow water. Like other finches, the bullfinch can be spotted bathing in rivers and ponds during hot summer weather.

The bullfinch is also skilled at picking out the seeds from fruit still on the tree, leaving the skin and pulp hanging.

Orkney and Shetland, which has become a popular destination for birdwatchers. These northern birds are very similar to their British counterparts. Populations in Europe and Asia are also partially migratory.

Decreasing population

Traditionally, bullfinches prefer to live in deciduous woodland, copses, thickets and dense, overgrown hedgerows on farmland. The birds also frequent parks, mature gardens and churchyards. Between 1967 and 1999, however, populations fell by 75 per cent on farmland and 40 per cent on woodland, and the decline continues.

Bullfinches are nearly always seen in pairs, providing an opportunity to compare the female's dull pink breast to the vibrant rose of the male. The pair form an unusually close bond, which can last for several years.

BULLFINCH CALENDAR

MARCH • MAY

Pairs establish small breeding territories, occasionally singing a very quiet, warbling song. The female builds a twiggy nest and incubates a clutch of eggs for about two weeks.

JUNE • AUGUST

The young leave the nest after 15–17 days but continue to be fed by their parents for a further two or three weeks. As the adults prepare for another brood, the chicks disperse.

SEPTEMBER • OCTOBER

Juveniles, fledglings and up to three broods of young swell the numbers of bullfinches seen at this time of year. Plenty of fruits and seeds provide rich pickings.

NOVEMBER • FEBRUARY

As food becomes harder to find, families split up. Pairs stay close together and may join up with other pairs. Loose groups may gather where food is more plentiful, such as in woodland clearings.

Falling numbers probably reflect the fact that many of the British birds live on or near agricultural land. Diminishing hedgerow and field margins, and fewer insects and plants resulting from increased use of agricultural sprays, have combined to remove much of the food and cover that many small birds and their young depend upon.

Reasons for the decline of the woodland population are less clear. It is possible that many woodland birds also depend upon local farmland for at least part of the year, and so have been similarly affected. A determination to curb the decline, not just of bullfinches but of several other birds and mammals, has led to hedgerow replanting and land stewardship grants.

WILDLIFE WATCH

Where can I see bullfinches?

● Although the bullfinch can be a difficult bird to find, especially now that its numbers have declined, a track with a good tall hedge on either side and woodlands nearby is a good option. Country walks on minor roads bordered by dense hedgerows are also worth trying.

● Listen for the bullfinch's low, piping calls and then watch carefully, especially if there is a gap in the hedge that a bird may fly across. Look for the distinctive white rump, contrasting with a black tail.

Recognising small warblers

Amid the foliage of woodland and scrub, these diminutive birds engage in almost ceaseless activity, foraging for insects. Telling them apart can be tricky but for their songs, which range from loud and musical to high-pitched and shrill.

The lively behaviour of these small birds makes it unusual to catch more than a fleeting glimpse of them, so identifying them can be something of a challenge. Those belonging to the genus *Phylloscopus* are known as leaf warblers, and the three most commonly seen in the British Isles are the willow warbler, chiffchaff and wood warbler. Closely related to the leaf warblers are the goldcrest and firecrest. These two have different colouring from the leaf warblers but are similar to each other.

Summer visitors

The willow warbler is a familiar migrant, arriving from its mainly African wintering grounds from late March and spreading out across Britain and Ireland, even where the shrub cover is sparse.

Most chiffchaffs arrive from southern Europe at around the same time, settling in woodland and hedgerows all over the country, although not many reach as far as the northern parts of Scotland. Small but increasing numbers of chiffchaffs also spend the winter in Britain, mainly near coasts in the south. These birds are sometimes joined by chiffchaffs from Europe.

Wood warblers arrive from Africa in April and May. They are not so numerous as the other leaf warblers and head mainly north and west.

Related crests

Goldcrests are resident in the British Isles and their numbers are swelled in winter by an influx from the Continent. They are mainly birds of coniferous forests but also

The dainty willow warbler can be found in woods and scrub throughout the summer. It is difficult to tell apart from the chiffchaff, except for its song.

breed in mixed woodland and mature conifer hedges in suburban settings, especially in areas where goldcrest numbers are high.

Firecrests are much rarer, mostly migrants, and confined to locations such as the New Forest in Hampshire, which is one of their breeding strongholds. In September and October, some birds are seen in migration hotspots such as Portland, Dungeness, Cley and the Scilly Isles.

WILDLIFE WATCH

Where can I see small warblers?

● Willow warblers and chiffchaffs both favour deciduous woodland, and frequently nest within earshot of one another. Chiffchaffs tend to prefer more mature woods whereas willow warblers are often found in patches of scrub. Willow warblers and chiffchaffs are present on their breeding territories from late March to August or September.

● Wood warblers nest in mature deciduous woodland, where beech or sessile oak predominates and there is

little or no ground cover. They are there from early April to August.

● Goldcrests breed mainly in conifer woodland. In winter they appear in mixed flocks in deciduous woodland.

● Firecrests are rare though increasing breeders in Britain, favouring mature conifers and mixed woodlands. They also nest in oak or beech woods where holly grows beneath the other trees. They visit the coast, and small numbers winter in southern England.

EASY GUIDE TO SPOTTING SMALL WARBLERS

Willow warbler

Chiffchaff

Wood warbler

Goldcrest

Firecrest

WHAT ARE SMALL WARBLERS?

● All warblers belong to the family Sylviidae. The leaf warblers, which include the willow warbler, chiffchaff and wood warbler, belong to the genus *Phylloscopus*.

● The goldcrest and firecrest, collectively known as crests, are classified separately in the genus *Regulus*. They are the smallest birds in Britain and Europe.

HOW CAN I IDENTIFY SMALL WARBLERS?

● Willow warblers and chiffchaffs are very similar in body shape and plumage colour. However, the willow warbler has pale brown legs, while the chiffchaff's are darker and greyer. The song of the willow warbler is a descending scale of clear sweet notes ending with a flourish, whereas the chiffchaff sings its name.

● Wood warblers have yellowish upperparts that contrast markedly with their white underparts. The main song is an accelerating trill.

● Goldcrests have olive brown upperparts and dingy white underparts. The crest is orange in males but golden in females. The voice is very high-pitched.

● Firecrests resemble goldcrests but have a black eyestripe and white eyebrow. The song is similar to, but shorter than, the goldcrest's.

Distribution map key

■ Present all year round

□ Present during summer months

□ Present during winter months

▨ Spring and autumn passage migrant

□ Not present

WILLOW WARBLER *Phylloscopus trochilus*

Plain, olive green upperparts contrast with the bird's yellowish white underparts. Its eyebrow is yellow and its chin white or very pale yellow. The bill is brown and the legs are pale orange-brown. As summer progresses, adults become browner above and whiter below through feather abrasion. Juveniles are much yellower.

● SIZE
Length 10.5–11.5cm (4–4½in)

● NEST
Grass cup with domed roof, built on ground in dense vegetation

● BREEDING
6–8 white, reddish brown finely speckled eggs laid in April–May

● FOOD
Mainly small insects and larvae

● HABITAT
Open, shrubby areas, copses and hedgerows, young plantations, woodland edges and clearings

The willow warbler is the most common summer visitor to Britain. It sometimes hovers to catch insects, but usually gleans its prey from shrub leaves.

● VOICE
Descending, sad musical song of liquid notes; distinctly two-syllabled *'hoo-eet'* calls

● DISTRIBUTION
Common summer visitor to most of Britain and Ireland

Olive green upperparts

Pale eyebrow

Yellowish white underparts

Pale orange-brown legs

Longer wings than those of the chiffchaff

CHIFFCHAFF *Phylloscopus collybita*

Similar to the willow warbler, the chiffchaff is distinguished by its song. Adults are brownish olive above and dull yellowish buff below, merging into buff on the flanks. The eyebrow is pale and the legs dark. Juveniles resemble adults, but are browner above and warmer yellow below. Northern and Siberian migrants are greyer.

● SIZE
Length 10–11cm (4–4¼in)

● NEST
Domed cup of grasses with fine lining, built just above ground level, in dense cover

● BREEDING
4–7 white, lightly spotted eggs laid in April–May

● FOOD
Mainly small insects and larvae

● HABITAT
Open woodland, copses and hedgerows

Unless it is heard singing, the chiffchaff is very difficult to distinguish from the willow warbler. It is a summer visitor to woods with dense undergrowth.

● VOICE
Persistent, rising in pitch, *'hweet hweet'* calls and monotonous *'chiff chaff chiff…'* song

● DISTRIBUTION
Common summer visitor to most of Britain and Ireland, less common in northern Scotland; small numbers overwinter in southern England

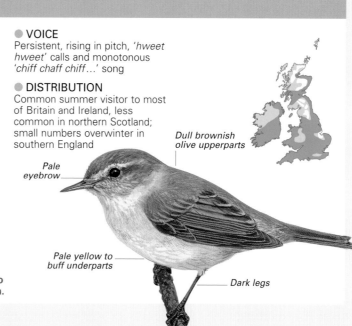

Dull brownish olive upperparts

Pale eyebrow

Pale yellow to buff underparts

Dark legs

WOOD WARBLER *Phylloscopus sibilatrix*

This colourful warbler is slightly larger than the willow warbler and chiffchaff, with yellow-green upperparts, a yellow eyebrow, throat and upper chest and white underparts. The browner tail and wings have yellowish feather margins. A dark upper mandible on the bill contrasts with a pale lower mandible. The legs are pale yellowish brown. Juveniles resemble adults.

● **SIZE**
Length 12–12.5cm (4½–4¾in)

● **NEST**
Domed cup of grasses and leaves, built on ground, often against a slope

● **BREEDING**
6–7 white, densely spotted eggs laid in May–June

● **FOOD**
Insects, larvae and spiders

● **HABITAT**
Mature open woods with a high canopy, especially sessile oak and beech, in hilly country

Most distinctive of all the leaf warblers, the wood warbler arrives in April and May and leaves again in July and August. The male has a butterfly-like territorial display.

● **VOICE**
Loud, sweet *'pew pew'*; song an elaboration of the *'pew pew'* call or a series of *'stip stip'* notes that accelerate to a shivering trill

● **DISTRIBUTION**
Summer visitor, mainly in northern and western Britain, very rare in Ireland

Yellowish green upperparts

Bright yellow throat and upper chest

Pure white belly and undertail coverts

GOLDCREST *Regulus regulus*

Europe's smallest bird, the goldcrest has a dumpy body, tiny bill, large eyes, short legs and wings. Its dull olive green upperparts have darker flight feathers and two white wingbars. The underparts are pale olive green. Males have an orange-yellow crown with black edging. Females have a yellow centre to the crown. Juveniles lack the colourful crown.

● **SIZE**
Length 9cm (3½in)

● **NEST**
Tiny cup of moss, lichens and cobwebs built near tip of conifer twig

● **BREEDING**
8–12 pale, finely speckled eggs laid in April–May; 2 broods

● **FOOD**
Tiny insects and spiders

● **HABITAT**
Mainly conifer woods when breeding, disperses more widely in winter

A pale area around its black eye gives the goldcrest a slightly surprised expression.

● **VOICE**
High-pitched *'tseee'* calls and rhythmic trilling song, beyond some people's hearing range

● **DISTRIBUTION**
Common resident across most of Britain and Ireland

Female

All-yellow crown

Golden crown, brighter in centre

Male

FIRECREST *Regulus ignicapillus*

The male has an orange-red and gold crown stripe bordered with black, a white eyebrow and black eyestripe. In the female, the crown is bright yellow. Bright olive green upperparts blend into bronze patches on the side of the neck. The firecrest's underparts are pale. Juveniles are similar in appearance to adults, but have no bright crown.

● **SIZE**
Length 9cm (3½in)

● **NEST**
Ball of mosses and lichens suspended beneath a twig at the end of a branch

● **BREEDING**
7–12 pale buff eggs marked with red dot, laid in March–May

● **FOOD**
Tiny insects and spiders

● **HABITAT**
Woodland, gardens, heathland and scrub

More brightly coloured than the similar goldcrest, the firecrest is secretive in its behaviour. It is a rare breeder in the south of Britain.

● **VOICE**
High-pitched *'zit zit'* calls, lower pitched than goldcrest, song very rapid and shrill

● **DISTRIBUTION**
Mainly a winter visitor to southern England, with scattered breeding records in the south

Bronze-coloured shoulder patch

Male has orange-red patch on gold crown

Broad white eyebrow and black eyestripe

Underparts paler than those of the goldcrest

The purple emperor

In mature woodlands of southern England, this spectacular butterfly emerges from its chrysalis to take up residence in the tree canopy. On summer mornings, the brilliantly coloured male flutters down to drink flower nectar.

The purple emperor is one of Britain's largest resident butterflies. The wingspan of the female may reach as much as 92mm (4in), while that of the male can be 78mm (3in). The blackish upperside – browner in the female – has a broad, white stripe across each wing, and a few white spots occur near the tip of the forewing. At the rear of each hind wing near the base there is an orange-ringed eyespot, and splashes of orange at the corners.

The brilliant purple sheen that gives the butterfly its name is exhibited by the male only. It is produced by the microscopic structure of the scales that cover the wings and not by a pigment. Sunlight striking the scales is partly absorbed so that only the violet end of the spectrum is reflected.

The underside of the wings reveals an attractive mixture of russet and silvery grey, and bears white markings similar to those on the upperside. Another prominent, orange-ringed eyespot is positioned close to the edge of each forewing.

The iridescence of the male purple emperor's wings is visible only when the butterfly holds them at a particular angle.

Early stages

Much of the purple emperor's life is spent developing from an egg to a caterpillar and then a chrysalis, before it emerges as an adult butterfly, after which it lives for about six weeks.

In late summer, the female leaves the tree canopy to lay her eggs singly on the upperside of low-growing goat or common willow leaves. The eggs hatch in about 10 days.

At first the tiny green caterpillars have round, black heads. As they grow and shed their skins, however, they develop the pair of distinctive pinkish tinged 'horns' that distinguish mature individuals.

The chrysalis is formed on the twig of a goat willow bush in June or July. It looks just like a young leaf and has markings that mimic the leaf's veins. It even hangs from the twig in a leaf-like manner.

LURING MALES

In the 19th century, naturalists discovered that male purple emperor butterflies can be coaxed from the tree tops by placing the rotting corpse of a small mammal or bird on a woodland path. They are also attracted by rabbit droppings and horse manure. The butterflies flutter down to drink the moisture from these morsels, which is a valuable source of sodium and other minerals essential for the healthy function of the butterflies' reproductive systems.

Purple emperors inhabit mature woodlands, especially those on heavy soils. Such woods are usually dominated by oaks, although the butterflies have no particular allegiance to these trees. They spend most of their time gliding around the tree tops and feeding on honeydew – partly digested tree sap exuded by aphids. The butterflies also drink sap oozing from wounded trees. Males sometimes drop to ground level to drink from muddy puddles. The females are seen much less often, although they do have to leave the canopy to lay their eggs on willow trees.

Breeding behaviour
During the afternoon, male purple emperors move to the highest point of their woodland home, which usually means that they gather on or around one of the tallest trees. This is known as the master tree. It is often referred to as the master oak, but it does not necessarily have to be an oak. Each male adopts a small territory, which may be no more than a cluster of twigs at the tip of a branch. The male defends this against rivals by flying at them and

Around 18 days after the chrysalis is formed, the adult butterfly emerges. At first, it can do little but cling to the leaf as its wings fill out and stiffen. As soon as it can fly, it flutters weakly to the safety of the canopy.

In July and August, in the mornings, a purple emperor will leave the canopy to feed on honeydew and tree sap. Later in the day, the butterflies return to the tree tops to defend territories.

engaging in short skirmishes before returning to its perch. Unmated females gravitate towards master trees and are immediately courted by the resident males. Mating takes place high in the canopy, often far from the master tree, and the female lays her eggs a day or two later.

The eggs are laid singly, usually on the leaves of goat willow or sometimes on those of common sallow that grows on the edges of woodland rides and clearings. After hatching, young caterpillars are very difficult to spot, because they are pale green and always rest on the mid-rib near the tip of the leaf. After the first moult or skin change, each caterpillar acquires a prominent pair of horns. No other British caterpillar has similar horns, although some moth larvae have horn-like tufts of hair.

Caterpillar transformation
After the second moult, the caterpillar hibernates. Responding to the short days of autumn and possibly the yellowing of leaves, the caterpillar turns brown. It settles on a twig – against a bud or in a fork – and spins a bed of silk on which it lies motionless and almost invisible for about five months. It wakes in April, when buds are starting to burst, and feeds for six weeks or so, moulting twice more.

When fully grown, usually by the middle of June, the caterpillar is about 4cm (1½in) long. It now turns into a pupa – or chrysalis – remaining at this stage for about two weeks. In early July it emerges as a butterfly and the whole cycle begins again.

The female purple emperor occasionally ventures down to ground level to drink. Larger than the male, she does not have the same iridescence but is a rich brown colour with similar markings.

WILDLIFE WATCH

Where can I see purple emperor butterflies?

● Look in mature woodlands in central and southern England, especially south of the Thames in Surrey, the Sussex Weald and Hampshire.

● Search from early July until the end of August in areas of mature oak, alongside goat willow bushes.

● Join an organised excursion. Contact Butterfly Conservation, Manor Yard, East Lulworth, Wareham, Dorset BH20 5QP (telephone 0870 774 4309) or visit www.butterfly-conservation.org.uk; also English Nature, Northminster House, Peterborough PE1 1UA (telephone 01733 455000) or visit www.english-nature.org.uk

The stag beetle

As dusk falls, a gentle buzzing sound heralds the presence of the largest by far of the British land beetles. The antler-like jaws of the male are a fearsome sight, but this unmistakable insect is entirely harmless to humans.

Male stag beetles behave aggressively towards each other during the mating season. Often they throw an opponent, showing how immensely strong they are for their size.

The wood-feeding stag beetle, a member of the family Lucanidae, has a long larval stage and a short but vigorous adult life. Its overgrown jaws, which nowadays play a more important role in mating rituals than in feeding, are its main identifying feature. Their similarity to antlers has provided the beetles with their common name. The male's jaws are too big for the muscles that should operate them. The beetles can hardly bring their tips together and cannot use them to bite. The female's jaws, although much smaller, are more powerful and she can close them so as to give a nip if handled.

Wrestling males

The male's jaws have evolved to be used in pre-mating behaviour. Two males interlock their 'antlers', and one male can even pick up and overturn another by grabbing it around the body. Although such fights occur commonly among captive stag beetles, they are rarely seen in the wild. When they do occur, they usually take place in the presence of a female, who is then carried off by the victor. After mating, she uses her spiny front legs to tunnel into tree stumps and other dead timber, including old, rotten fence posts, where she lays clusters of large yellowish eggs, usually at or below ground level. Oak is the preferred timber, but elm, beech and ash are also used, and stumps of apple trees in orchards and gardens are sometimes taken over.

PROTECTED!

In 1998, the Wildlife and Countryside Act was revised and stag beetles are now granted partial protection. They may not, for example, be offered for sale to collectors.

The oversized jaws are not the sign of a carnivorous predator. Adult stag beetles consume only tree sap or fruit. In fact, this stage of their lives is so short that many probably do not feed at all.

Summer beetles

Adult beetles emerge from their chrysalises in early summer to feed on sap oozing from trees and also on ripe fruit. They are attracted to lights and can sometimes be found crawling dazedly on pavements beneath street lamps.

Both sexes may grow from 3 to 7.5cm (1 to 3in) long, including their jaws, although many females are much smaller. The size attained by the adult beetle depends largely on the quality of the timber eaten during the larval stage. Undersized males may have disproportionately small jaws, not much larger than those of a female.

The head and thorax are black, but the elytra, or wing cases, are dark purplish brown or dark chestnut brown. The male's antlers are often reddish in tone.

From June to August, the beetles take to the wing, usually at dusk, in a fast, buzzing flight. Although both sexes fly, most of the airborne insects are males searching for mates. The females are more likely to stay on the ground.

Stag beetles are much less common today than they were a century ago, largely because they are losing their favoured habitats. Modern forestry practice and gardening habits are not good for stag beetles. Old tree stumps are rarely left to rot and timber fence posts and gate posts are treated to deter insect attack. In addition to this, many posts are

made of metal or concrete. Dutch elm disease, while a disaster for trees, provided an abundance of dead stumps and the beetles flourished for a while, but this source of food is running out. Despite these setbacks, the beetle is still relatively common in some places, especially in and around London, where parks have plenty of old trees for them to lay their eggs.

BROWN-HEADED LARVAE

Stag beetle eggs hatch after a few weeks and the larvae immediately start to chew the rotting wood in which they find themselves, with their large jaws. The larva has a brown head and its plump white body is always curved in a 'C' shape. Although it has six well-developed legs at the front, it is a lethargic creature and remains out of sight in the tunnel that it chews out for itself. Larvae are occasionally found when old stumps and logs are being cut up, and if handled they sometimes emit a brief rattling sound produced by rubbing the back and middle legs together.

Wood is not easily digested and the larva relies on an army of bacteria in its gut. It takes four to six years to mature because wood is not particularly nutritious. The fully grown larva is up to 8cm (3in) long, and will eventually chew its way out of the timber to pupate in the surrounding soil.

The fully grown larva is about the length of a human index finger. The stag beetle exists for the vast majority of its life in this stage, growing slowly.

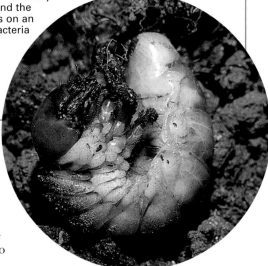

▲ Always prominent, the male stag beetle's jaws are emphasised by their red colour. Legend once had it that the male could carry a live coal in its jaws, and was responsible for setting house roofs on fire.

WILDLIFE WATCH

Where can I see stag beetles?

● Stag beetles are confined to southern counties in England, with their most northerly outpost probably in Norfolk.

● Ancient woodlands, such as the New Forest, and parkland with old trees are good places in which to search. The beetles are still abundant in suburban London.

● The People's Trust for Endangered Species launched a 'Great Stag Hunt' in September 2005, a survey designed to update knowledge of the beetle's status by finding out where they live and how many there are. The results will update a similar census carried out in 1998.

▲ Although the female is smaller than the male and her jaws are much shorter, they are strong and may be used for defence against mice, frogs or blackbirds.

▶ A few weeks in summer are wholly devoted to reproducing – males fly in search of mates and females then search for rotten wood in which to lay their eggs. After that, the adults die.

Blood-red ants

On a hot, sunny day, raiding parties of these large ants may invade the nests of related species, seizing cocoons to eat or to carry back to their colony to raise as workers of their own.

Among ants, capturing the young of another species in order to enlarge the workforce is unusual behaviour in Britain. The now rather rare blood-red or slave-making ant, *Formica sanguinea*, is adept at it. In late summer, blood-red ants can be seen marching purposefully back across heathland or open woodland, some carrying cocoons, the objective of their raid on another ants nest.

Formica sanguinea, a large species – workers are about 1cm (½in) long – nests in the ground, sometimes under logs and stones, but usually in tree stumps. It is an aggressive ant and any attempt to disturb the nest is met with formidable defence – a barricade of gaping jaws and a barrage of formic acid shot from the rear ends of the workers.

Plunder and pillage

Blood-red ants obtain most of their slaves from the nests of the closely related species *Formica fusca* and the rare *Formica rubifarbis*, although they will occasionally take wood ants, *Formica rufa*, as slaves. Blood-red ants travel up to about 100m (300ft) in search of targets. Days beforehand, scouts investigate the earmarked nest, and the raid begins with the ants leaving their colony in small groups. There is no mass exodus and certainly nothing resembling the marauding columns formed by the army ants and driver ants of tropical regions.

The groups gradually link up to surround the target nest. *F. fusca* itself is a relatively fearsome insect, but it is no match for the slave-makers and does not attempt to defend its nest. *F. fusca* workers simply pick up as many of their own grubs

and pupal cocoons as they can save and scurry off to a safe distance, leaving the raiders to plunder the rest.

The slave raiders probably spray the *F. fusca* nest with powerful scents that alarm the resident ants and cause them to scatter. This is certainly what happens with some American slave-makers. The scents linger for several hours but eventually disperse, and the residents return to their ransacked nest.

The blood-red ants consume some of the stolen pupae and take the rest back to their own nest. In due course, the *F. fusca* workers are allowed to emerge from their

All the worker ants in a colony are sterile females, so they do not produce their own young. They strive together to defend the nest against other ants and provide food for the grubs and their mother, the queen.

The blood-red ant is immensely strong and can carry slave grubs and cocoons as big as itself back to the nest. When these hatch, they become slave workers.

Like many of its relatives, the blood-red ant often covers its nest with a pile of leaf litter and other debris. However, the mounds are never as large as those of the more common wood ant.

cocoons unharmed and are integrated into the blood-red workforce. They are restricted to maintenance tasks – they probably do not forage for food and they certainly do not go on slave-raids.

Blood-red ants can exist without slaves, but they do need *F. fusca* to start a nest. The blood-red queen cannot build her own, so she invades an established *F. fusca* one. She usually chooses a small one with few workers and appropriates a batch of cocoons. These she cares for and defends against the other occupants of the nest.

The workers that emerge from the captive cocoons are bonded to the blood-red queen and work for her. Their first task is to kill the reigning *F. fusca* queen – their own mother. This stops any more *F. fusca* eggs being laid in the colony, and the blood-red queen promptly lays a new batch. These and the resulting grubs are cared for by the *F. fusca* workers, but hatch as blood-red workers. The colony becomes a mixture of the two species for a while, until the *F. fusca* workers die out and the nest is populated entirely by blood-red ants. This process is known as temporary social parasitism.

Willing slaves

Although commonly referred to as slaves, *F. fusca* workers live in much the same way as they would in their own nest, apart from the fact that they do not seem to forage outside. They are merely working for a different mistress of another species.

Although the blood-red ant is the only one of 50 or so British ant species that carries out slave-raids, it is not the only one to employ slave labour. *Strongylognathus testaceus* is a tiny brown ant, about 2mm (⅛in) long, which relies on the larger turf ant *Tetramorium*

Older worker ants forage on behalf of the rest of the colony. They share any food with the younger ants – their main task is to care for the queen and the grubs.

caespitum to do most of its work. The young, mated *S. testaceus* queen enters the *T. caespitum* nest and lives alongside the resident queen. Both females lay eggs, but the *T. caespitum* queen produces workers only, which undertake the chores in the mixed colony. Nearly all the eggs of the *S. testaceus* queen give rise to males and new queens. The few workers that are produced do little or no work in the colony. The large jaws of these ants suggest that they once indulged in slave-raiding, but this no longer occurs and the species has now adopted an almost completely parasitic lifestyle.

Raiding party

Blood-red ants kidnap pupae from the nests of related species, carrying them away in their huge jaws. Later, the emerging adults are used to swell the nest's workforce. A colony may contain up to half a million individuals.

Long legs help the blood-red ants to negotiate any obstacles blocking their path.

A steady stream of workers wend their way to and from the raided nest. Those on the return journey struggle with their heavy burdens.

Recognising smaller deciduous trees

Among oaks, beeches and other stately trees, the smaller deciduous trees are often overlooked. Yet they are a familiar part of the woodland scene, and it is rewarding to identify the most common yet less familiar species.

The large trees of mixed woodland are readily recognisable. They include both oaks – pedunculate and sessile – along with ash, beech and silver birch. Although these five trees may exhibit many differences, they share an important characteristic – where conditions suit them, they can dominate a wooded landscape. They frequently appear to do this in stands of only one type of tree.

However, although it might seem that the larger trees in a woodland are growing to the exclusion of other, less vigorous types, this is rarely the case. Dominant trees actually form a framework within which a number of smaller trees can thrive.

Growing habits

Many smaller woodland trees require specific conditions. Any mixed deciduous woodland is therefore unlikely to hold more than three or four of them. It does, however, mean that the trees are common where suitable conditions prevail. Field maple, for example, grows in many areas but flourishes on lime-rich soil, and so is prevalent on chalk downland in southern and eastern Britain. The hardiness of rowan trees has led to them being widely planted in more severe climates, especially the Scottish Highlands. A relative of the rowan, the wild service tree, grows in hedgerows and ancient woodland in western England and Wales, and clay soils in southern and eastern England.

Like all other deciduous trees, the smaller woodland species shed their leaves in autumn. Many grow from a single trunk, but several can be multi-stemmed. However, the appearance of small deciduous trees is often influenced by the way in which particular woodlands are managed. For example, hazel is often coppiced to produce numerous growing stems.

Most deciduous woodland trees thrive in the planted hedgerows that are a counterpart of natural clearings and woodland edges.

New locations

Deciduous woodland trees produce fruits, seeds and nuts that are transported in many ways, including by the wind and in bird droppings. As well as these natural means of spreading to new places, deciduous trees have been planted by humans. Some are planted because they are economically valuable while others make excellent hedging material.

◄ **With its roots clinging to rocks, and only a toehold in shallow soil, this rowan – or mountain ash – looks precarious. However, the tree has a tenacious grip that allows it to grow in many places, whether overhanging woodland rivers or in rugged, upland regions.**

EASY GUIDE TO SPOTTING SMALLER DECIDUOUS TREES

Field maple

Black poplar

Hazel

Bird cherry

Sycamore

Aspen

Wild service tree

Rowan or mountain ash

Common whitebeam

Bird cherry is often planted as an ornamental tree for its long, hanging bunches of black and red cherries. These are very bitter, however, and edible only to birds.

HOW CAN I IDENTIFY SMALLER DECIDUOUS TREES?

● Study all the parts of the tree, including its bark, flowers, catkins if present, fruits and seeds, to confirm any tentative identification. It may be necessary to mark the site of the tree on a map, and return later in the season.

● Leaf shape is an important guide. The discovery of a mystery leaf on the woodland floor can often indicate the presence of a previously undiscovered tree. In the autumn, leaves are often a distinct colour.

● Look at the shape and colour of winter buds.

● Generally, look at specific features that are consistent in members of the same family. The overall shape of the tree is of little help in identifying it. Not only is it often difficult to see the outline in a dense wooded setting, but each tree is likely to be different from another of its kind growing somewhere else. Surrounding trees affect its shape, as does the amount of shade cast by the canopy of larger trees. Trees in a hedgerow setting are often pruned or cut back, so their natural shape is not obvious. Visit an arboretum or park where deciduous trees may be labelled.

WILDLIFE WATCH

Where can I see smaller deciduous trees?

● Many natural and semi-natural woodlands across Britain support small deciduous trees. Each region is likely to have four or five particular trees that are most common since conditions suit them. Some are deliberately planted in urban settings, either for their attractive foliage or for spring flowers.

● Field maple, hazel and aspen all grow wild in Britain in many woodlands and hedgerows around the country.

● Black poplar, bird cherry and wild service trees are mainly found in particular areas where the conditions suit their growing requirements.

● Mountain ash is most common in western and upland areas. Aspen and sycamore are widely planted, the latter having been introduced to Britain.

FIELD MAPLE *Acer campestre*

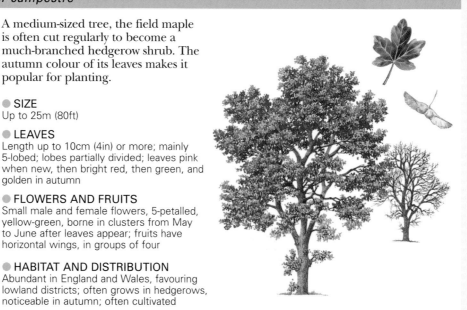

A medium-sized tree, the field maple is often cut regularly to become a much-branched hedgerow shrub. The autumn colour of its leaves makes it popular for planting.

● SIZE
Up to 25m (80ft)

● LEAVES
Length up to 10cm (4in) or more; mainly 5-lobed; lobes partially divided; leaves pink when new, then bright red, then green, and golden in autumn

● FLOWERS AND FRUITS
Small male and female flowers, 5-petalled, yellow-green, borne in clusters from May to June after leaves appear; fruits have horizontal wings, in groups of four

● HABITAT AND DISTRIBUTION
Abundant in England and Wales, favouring lowland districts; often grows in hedgerows, noticeable in autumn; often cultivated

At the woodland's edge, field maple may grow into a medium-sized tree.

BLACK POPLAR *Populus nigra*

Black poplars often stand head and shoulders above nearby scrub trees.

Rather patchily distributed around Britain, the black poplar grows wild and is also cultivated. It is seldom found far from water. Forming an attractive, spreading tree, it has a domed crown when mature.

● SIZE
Up to 33m (108ft)

● LEAVES
Length 5–7.5cm (2–3in); almost triangular, but with rounded base and long stalk; surfaces shiny, and margin toothed

● FLOWERS AND FRUITS
Male catkins pendulous and reddish brown; female catkins green; both appear in March–April

● HABITAT AND DISTRIBUTION
Favours heavy, often damp, alluvial soils; mature trees common in parts of East Midlands and East Anglia; usually along hedgerow or fence boundaries

HAZEL *Corylus avellana*

A frequent shrub of the woodland understorey, the common hazel is also abundant in hedgerows. It is easy to overlook where it grows thinly, except in late winter when the catkins ripen.

● SIZE
Up to 6m (20ft)

● LEAVES
Length 5–12cm (2–4¾in); rounded-oval with heart-shaped base; yellow in autumn; margins double-toothed, upper surface downy

● FLOWERS AND FRUITS
Male catkins short, green from October onwards, yellow and pendulous by spring; female flowers tiny and bud-like with red styles at top, appear January to March

● HABITAT AND DISTRIBUTION
Widespread and often planted in hedgerows and woodlands where traditional woodland practices such as coppicing are followed

Periodic coppicing produces an array of tall, thin stems in hazel clumps.

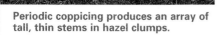

BIRD CHERRY *Prunus padus*

An elegant tree with smooth, dark purplish brown bark, the bird cherry grows best in pockets of damp soil. The blossom creates a stunning display for a few days in spring.

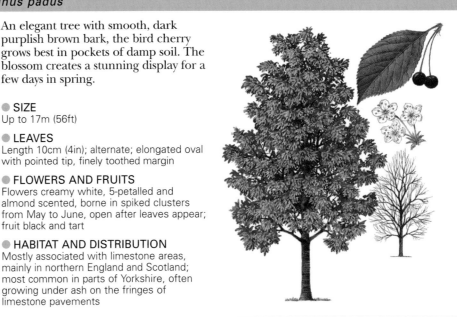

● SIZE
Up to 17m (56ft)

● LEAVES
Length 10cm (4in); alternate; elongated oval with pointed tip, finely toothed margin

● FLOWERS AND FRUITS
Flowers creamy white, 5-petalled and almond scented, borne in spiked clusters from May to June, open after leaves appear; fruit black and tart

● HABITAT AND DISTRIBUTION
Mostly associated with limestone areas, mainly in northern England and Scotland; most common in parts of Yorkshire, often growing under ash on the fringes of limestone pavements

In spring, bird cherry is a mass of flowers, buzzing with insect life.

SYCAMORE *Acer pseudoplatanus*

An introduced tree, the sycamore has an open, straggly shape. The bark is pinkish grey and smooth until the tree is about 80 years old. Then it splits, with patches peeling to reveal orange-brown.

● SIZE
Up to 35m (115ft)

● LEAVES
Length up to 25cm (10in), 5-lobed, with toothed margins; younger specimens have more dissected leaves

● FLOWERS AND FRUITS
Clusters of pendulous, yellow flowers appear after leaves first open on 10cm (4in) long stalks; fruits paired and two-winged; wings sharp-angled

● HABITAT AND DISTRIBUTION
Native to central Europe, but widely planted throughout Britain and often naturalised; invasive; its heavy leaf fall smothers many wild flowers

The sycamore grows vigorously whether solitary or in mixed woodlands.

ASPEN *Populus tremula*

A smallish tree with tall, tapering trunk, smooth, greyish brown bark and open crown, the aspen's fluttering leaves rustle in the breeze.

● SIZE
Up to 20m (66ft)

● LEAVES
Rounded to oval, rounded teeth around margin, dark green above, paler below; downy on opening but soon become hairless; turn golden-yellow for few days in autumn

● FLOWERS AND FRUITS
Catkins 8cm (3in) long, borne in terminal clusters from February to April; reddish male catkins and green female catkins on separate trees; both have dense white hairs

● HABITAT AND DISTRIBUTION
Native and widespread in Britain, favouring damp, poor soils; mature trees frequently surrounded by many small ones

Aspen often flourishes in groves, thanks to its ability to produce suckers.

WILD SERVICE TREE *Sorbus torminalis*

This spreading tree has a domed crown when mature. The bark, greyish brown at first, becomes fissured into blackish brown squares. The leaves turn red in autumn.

- **SIZE**
Up to 27m (89ft)

- **LEAVES**
Roughly oval, with 3 to 5 pairs of pointed lobes and serrated margin

- **FLOWERS AND FRUITS**
Flowers creamy white, 1.5cm (⅝in) across, borne in clusters, appear in May; fruit brown and round, about 1cm (½in) long

- **HABITAT AND DISTRIBUTION**
Native and widespread in England only; local and usually associated with ancient woodlands; favours heavy, often clay soils

Wild service trees achieve quite stately proportions if sheltered by larger trees.

ROWAN OR MOUNTAIN ASH *Sorbus aucuparia*

The rowan's bark is silvery grey and smooth with horizontal streaks, known as lenticels or breathing pores. It is often coated with lichens and mosses in unpolluted areas.

- **SIZE**
Up to 20m (66ft)

- **LEAVES**
Compound and pinnate, resembling those of ash; comprise 5–8 pairs of elongated oval, toothed leaflets, 5cm (2in) or so long

- **FLOWERS AND FRUITS**
Flowers creamy white, 5-petalled, produced in dense, flat-topped clusters in May; fruits rounded, bright red berries, borne in clusters in autumn

- **HABITAT AND DISTRIBUTION**
Widespread throughout most of Britain and Ireland, but characteristic of upland areas and acid soils; also widely planted in urban areas for its colourful berries

In late summer and autumn, bright red berries cover the whole tree.

COMMON WHITEBEAM *Sorbus aria*

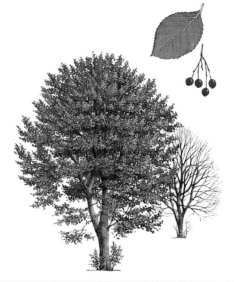

A spreading shrub with upswept branches, whitebeam has smooth, grey bark that develops a few fissures with age. The leaves have silvery white undersides.

- **SIZE**
Up to 25m (80ft)

- **LEAVES**
Vary from narrowly to broadly oval, up to 12cm (4¾in) long with irregular teeth around margin; green, under surface whitish and hairy

- **FLOWERS AND FRUITS**
Clusters of creamy white or pinkish flowers in May; fruits ovoid, bright orange-red

- **HABITAT AND DISTRIBUTION**
Native on wood and scrub, and especially inland chalk and limestone soils in parts of southern England; scarce but sown by birds farther north; planted in places

In spring, common whitebeams are covered in sprays of white flowers.

Forget-me-nots

The delicate flowers of tiny forget-me-nots are a familiar feature of many gardens. Several species also grow wild in Britain and Ireland, freckling the countryside with splashes of glorious blue.

The forget-me-nots are annual or perennial members of the comfrey and borage family, the Boraginaceae. As with many other members of this family, their wheel-shaped flowers are mostly blue – a relatively unusual colour in British native flora. Forget-me-nots also have the simple, undivided leaves that are typical of the family, and are hairy or bristly all over. Some are plants of wet or shady places, while others grow on dry, open ground.

The forget-me-not flower has a calyx of five hairy sepals, joined near the base. The petals are fused into a short tube, with five conspicuous, spreading lobes. Usually pink in bud, the petals are pale or bright blue in all species, except changing forget-me-not in which they are cream or yellowish when they first open. At the centre is an orange or yellow 'eye'.

Scorpion flowers

The inflorescences, or flower clusters, of all forget-me-nots are short and condensed in bud. However, the main stalk lengthens and curves as individual flowers mature. The resulting pattern is characteristic of the whole family and is reminiscent of the curled tail of a scorpion – hence the flowers' original name of scorpion-grasses.

The name forget-me-not did not gain popularity until the Romantic movement in the arts, during the early 19th century.

The flower clusters elongate in fruit. The fruit comprises four shiny, flattened nutlets (little nuts), often with a pronounced rim, enclosed deep within the calyx. Each nutlet contains a single seed.

Most forget-me-nots are found all over the British Isles and several are extremely common. A cultivar of wood forget-me-not is the spring-flowering plant found in many gardens. The wild plant has a limited range, being found mainly in eastern England and southern Scotland, but the

The field forget-me-not is common on arable and waste ground and in woodland rides throughout Britain. This hairy-leaved plant flowers from early April to September.

garden form often escapes to nearby waste ground and waysides.

Some species are scarcer. The *Red Data Book* of Britain's rarest wild plants lists the Alpine forget-me-not, which can be seen only on mountains in Scotland and northern England where it grows on rocky ledges and limestone grassland. The Jersey forget-me-not is restricted in northern Europe to Jersey in the Channel Islands and north-western France.

Early forget-me-not is a particularly small member of the family. Its soft-haired leaves and tiny, bright blue flowers decorate open areas throughout lowland Britain and a few places in Ireland from April to June.

Wood forget-me-not is found in upland woods in eastern England and southern Scotland, where it blankets the ground with a carpet of azure blue.

FORGET-ME-NOT FACT FILE

● Water forget-me-not
Myosotis scorpioides
Habitat and distribution
Common on wet ground
Size Up to 30cm (12in) tall,
sometimes 70cm (28in)
Key features
A creeping perennial, covered
with hairs closely appressed
(flattened against the stem and
leaves); leaves pale green,
stalkless, oblong; flowers bright
blue, occasionally pink or white,
8–13mm (^{3}/$_8$–^{5}/$_8$in) across, flat,
lobes slightly notched; fruit
stalks up to twice as long as
calyx; calyx teeth short,
triangular
Flowering time
June–September

● Tufted forget-me-not
Myosotis laxa
Habitat and distribution
Widespread beside ponds,
streams and canals
Size 20–50cm (8–20in) tall
Key features
A tufted annual or biennial with
appressed hairs, no runners;
leaves stalkless, oblong; flowers
bright blue, 3–5mm (^{1}/$_8$in–^{1}/$_4$in)
across, flat, lobes un-notched;
fruit stalks 2–3 times as long as
the calyx; calyx teeth spear-
shaped, pointed
Flowering time
May–August

● Wood forget-me-not
Myosotis sylvatica
Habitat and distribution
Woods, mainly in eastern
England, and garden escape;
rare in northern Scotland,
in north-east only in Ireland
Size 10–50cm (4–20in) tall
Key features
A biennial or short-lived
perennial, stems and leaves
with soft hairs; lower leaves
almost stalkless, oblong; flowers
pale blue, 6–10mm (^{1}/$_4$–^{3}/$_8$in)
across, flat; fruit stalks 1–2
times as long as calyx; calyx has
hooked hairs; fruits brown
Flowering time
April–July

● Alpine forget-me-not
Myosotis alpestris
Habitat and distribution
Rare on lime-rich, rocky
grassland in mountains of north
Pennines and Perthshire
Size 5–25cm (2–10in) tall
Key features
A tufted perennial, lower leaves
long-stalked; flowers bright blue,
fragrant; fruit stalks as long as
densely silvery haired calyx;
fruits black, shiny
Flowering time
June–August

● Creeping forget-me-not
Myosotis secunda
Habitat and distribution
Wet, lime-poor, upland soil
Size Up to 60cm (24in) long
Key features
A leafy, creeping perennial,
lower stems with spreading
hairs; leaves stalkless, oblong;
flowers bright blue, 4–8 mm
(^{1}/$_8$–^{3}/$_8$in) across, lobes slightly
notched, style very short; fruit
stalks 3–5 times as long as
calyx; calyx teeth long, pointed
Flowering time
May–August

● Jersey forget-me-not
Myosotis sicula
Habitat and distribution
Wet ground between sand
dunes in Jersey
Size 5–20cm (2–8in) tall
Key features
Similar to tufted forget-me-not,
semi-prostrate annual; flowers
2–3mm (^{1}/$_8$in) across, saucer-
shaped; calyx hairless, with
blunt teeth
Flowering time
May–June

● Pale forget-me-not
Myosotis stolonifera
Habitat and distribution
Wet ground in mountains of
northern England and southern
Scotland
Size 20–30cm (8–12in) tall
Key features
Similar to creeping forget-me-
not, stems with appressed hairs;
leaves bluish green, oval, twice
as long as broad; flowers pale
blue, 4–6mm (^{1}/$_8$–^{1}/$_4$in) across
Flowering time
June–August

Water forget-me-not
Myosotis scorpioides

Pale forget-me-not
Myosotis stolonifera

The Alpine forget-me-not is found
on Appleby Fells and Upper
Teesdale in northern England and
Ben Lawers in southern Scotland.
Short, open turf and steep rock
ledges are dotted with its tiny blue
flowers in June and July.

Tufted forget-me-not
Myosotis laxa

Jersey forget-me-not
Myosotis sicula

Wood forget-me-not
Myosotis sylvatica

Creeping forget-me-not
Myosotis secunda

Alpine forget-me-not
Myosotis alpestris

**Changing forget-me-not or
yellow and blue forget-me-not**
Myosotis discolor

**Field forget-me-not or
common forget-me-not**
Myosotis arvensis

Early forget-me-not
Myosotis ramosissima

FORGET-ME-NOT FACT FILE

● **Field forget-me-not or
common forget-me-not**
Myosotis arvensis
Habitat and distribution
Open woods, disturbed or
cultivated ground and sand
dunes; the most common wild
forget-me-not
Size 5–25cm (2–10in) tall,
sometimes 40cm (16in)
Key features
A softly greyish, hairy annual
or short-lived perennial; lower
leaves in loose rosette,
stalked, oblong; flowers blue,
2–5mm (1/8–1/4in) across,
saucer-shaped; fruit-stalks 2–3
times as long as bell-shaped
calyx; calyx with hooked hairs;
fruits dark brown or black
Flowering time
April–October

● **Changing forget-me-not
or yellow and blue forget-
me-not**
Myosotis discolor
Habitat and distribution
Locally common on heaths,
dry banks, waysides and
sandy, cultivated ground; in
the north on wet ground
between dunes and other
damp places
Size 5–25cm (2–10in) tall
Key features
A slender annual; leaves spear-
shaped or oblong; flowers
yellow or cream, turning blue,
1–2mm (1/8in) across, saucer-
shaped; fruit stalks shorter
than calyx, which has erect
teeth and hooked hairs
Flowering time
May–September

● **Early forget-me-not**
Myosotis ramosissima
Habitat and distribution
Common on heaths, dry
banks, light, cultivated soils;
bare, rocky places and sand
dunes
Size 2–25cm (3/4–10in) tall
Key features
A slender, often sprawling,
branched annual; leaves
spear-shaped or oblong;
flowers 1–3mm (1/8in) across,
bright blue, saucer-shaped;
fruit stalks 2–3 times as long
as calyx; calyx teeth spreading
in fruit
Flowering time
April–June

WILDLIFE WATCH

Where do
forget-me-nots
grow?

● About half the species of
forget-me-nots occur in
marshes, on pond edges and
streamsides and in the clearings
and rides of wet woodlands.

● Field forget-me-not, changing
forget-me-not and early forget-
me-not grow on dry, open
ground, such as sandy fields,
heaths and sand dunes.

● Pale forget-me-not grows by
upland streams and on wet
ground in northern Britain.
Creeping forget-me-not is most
common in wet upland areas.

Climbers and scramblers

Honeysuckle, bindweeds and bryonies, using sturdier plants for support, adorn hedgerows and woodlands with their flowers and berries. While some spread by entwining themselves around other foliage, others creep along open ground.

In order to reach the light that they need to survive, some plants have developed the habit of climbing towards it through the leaves and branches of other plants. Sometimes, they scramble and creep horizontally, even along the ground. Many plants of the tropical rainforest use these strategies and they have also been adopted in the temperate woodlands and waysides of Britain and Ireland by about a dozen native wild flowers and shrubs.

Bindweeds and honeysuckle twine their stems around another plant while the bryonies use clinging tendrils to climb higher. Each species twines in one direction only. For example, the black bryony grasps its host in a clockwise direction while the field and hedge bindweeds progress anti-clockwise.

Ivy attaches itself to either plants or man-made structures, including fences and walls, by putting out hundreds of tiny roots, while traveller's joy has developed another method of climbing, using special leaf stalks. Its woody stems hang from the woodland canopy in great loops, resembling the lianas of a jungle.

Native climbers, especially ivy and honeysuckle, are among the most distinctive and prominent of wild plants and are a major feature of woodlands and hedgerows. Their berries add a splash of colour to the late summer and autumn scene. The fruits of the bryonies are poisonous to humans. In contrast, other climbing plants have featured in British diets for centuries. The fruits of the hop are a traditional flavouring and preservative for beer, while the seeds of black bindweed are thought to have been harvested as a starchy food during prehistoric times.

Honeysuckle flowers profusely in locations with plenty of light, such as hedgerows. In gloomy woodland settings its blooms are less abundant.

◄ In autumn, the wispy seed heads of traveller's joy adorn hedgerows on calcareous soils in southern Britain, and account for its alternative name of old man's beard.

▼ Although considered a weed by many gardeners, hedge bindweed is one of the most attractive wayside flowers.

Family connections

Native climbers are drawn from several different families. Hop is a member of the family Cannabaceae, which also includes hemp. Traveller's joy is a woody member of the buttercups, with which it shares the feature of having numerous stamens and single-seeded fruits. It is also Britain's only native *Clematis*.

Black bindweed and copse bindweed belong to the dock and knotweed family. This group can be recognised by the little sock-like sheaths that cover the point on the stem where the leaves arise. Despite their shared name, the other four bindweeds – field, hedge, large and sea – are members of the convolvulus family, a large group of climbing or shrubby plants with showy bell-shaped flowers.

Honeysuckles belong to the same small family as elder and guelder rose. White bryony is related to marrows, melons and cucumbers. Black bryony, quite unrelated to the white, is Britain's only native yam.

Ivy, a tenacious climber, is the only member found in Britain of a mainly tropical family. Clinging harmlessly to broad-leaved trees, it provides nectar for wasps and flies and berries for birds.

Most of these climbing plants are found all over the country in abundance. However, the two bryonies are plants of southern Europe, and in the British Isles they are almost entirely restricted to England and Wales. Copse bindweed is a rare plant now, found only in central southern England. Its decline is probably a consequence of a reduction in the traditional practice of rotational cutting of hedges and coppices.

The small, rare fly honeysuckle, a shrub or sometimes a scrambler rather than a true climber, is at the very edge of its range in Britain and grows in just a few sites on the South Downs in West Sussex.

CLIMBERS FACT FILE

● Hop
Humulus lupulus
Habitat and distribution
Twining and trailing on hedges, shrubs, trees and fences, widespread, usually an escape from cultivation, but native in damp woods in the south
Size 3–8m (9ft 10in–26ft 3in) tall
Key features
Roughly hairy perennial; stems 4-angled; leaves in opposite pairs, 3–5 lobed, up to 10cm (4in) long; flowers male or female in greenish, hanging clusters, the female cone-like in fruit, clothed in pale green papery scales
Flowering time
June–September

● Traveller's joy or old man's beard
Clematis vitalba
Habitat and distribution
Scrambles over hedges, scrub and banks, up into trees; common on chalk and limestone soils north to North Wales and the Midlands and along coast into south-east Scotland; all over Ireland except far north
Size Up to 30m (100ft) tall
Key features
Woody perennial; leaves in opposite pairs, compound with usually 5 stalks and paired leaflets, often toothed; flowers in clusters, each with 4 greenish cream sepals and cream stamens; fruit single-seeded, with feathery plumes
Flowering time
July–September

● Black bindweed
Fallopia convolvulus
Habitat and distribution
Common in cultivated and rich soils
Size 10–120cm (4–48in) tall
Key features
Prostrate or twining annual; pointed leaves heart or arrow-shaped; flowers, greenish white or pinkish, in clusters; fruit 3–5mm (⅛–¼in) long, triangular, matt black, enclosed in flower remains
Flowering time
June–October

● Copse bindweed
Fallopia dumetorum
Habitat and distribution
Rare and decreasing in woodland margins, coppice and hedgerows on well-drained soils in parts of central south England
Size 1–2m (3–6½ft) tall
Key features Similar to black bindweed, but taller and more robust, with shiny fruits enclosed in winged flower remains
Flowering time
June–September

● Field bindweed or bindweed
Convolvulus arvensis
Habitat and distribution
Common in cultivated and waste ground, trailing and climbing on hedges and wire fences
Size 30–200cm (12–80in)
Key features
Prostrate or twining, often hairy, perennial with extensive root system; leaves spear or arrow-shaped; flowers funnel-shaped, 10–25mm (⅜–1in) across, white, pink or pink-and-white, without inflated sepal-like bracts at base; fruit small, 2-celled, spherical capsule
Flowering time
June–September

● Hedge bindweed or bellbine
Calystegia sepium
Habitat and distribution
Common in hedgerows, scrubby waste ground, wood margins and marshes
Size 1–3m (3–10ft) or more tall
Key features Larger plant than field bindweed, hairless perennial with extensive fleshy roots; leaves heart- or arrow-shaped, pointed; flowers funnel-shaped, 30–60mm (1¼–2⅜in) across, white, pink with fine white stripes (especially in Ireland), with a pair of slightly inflated sepal-like bracts at their base; fruit 2-celled capsule enclosed by the bracts
Flowering time
June–September

Hop
Humulus lupulus

Traveller's joy or old man's beard
Clematis vitalba

Copse bindweed
Fallopia dumetorum

Black bindweed
Fallopia convolvulus

Field bindweed or bindweed
Convolvulus arvensis

Hedge bindweed or bellbine
Calystegia sepium

CLIMBERS FACT FILE

● **Large bindweed or American bellbine**
Calystegia silvatica
Habitat and distribution
Abundant in untended gardens, on hedges and fences
Size 1–4m (3–13ft) or more tall
Key features
Similar to hedge bindweed but more robust and leafy; flowers 60–90mm (2⅜–3½in) across, white, with a pair of strongly inflated sepal-like bracts at their base
Flowering time
June–October

● **Fly honeysuckle**
Lonicera xylosteum
Habitat and distribution
Very rare in a few places on lime-rich soil in woods on the South Downs, occasionally naturalised elsewhere
Size 1–2m (3–6½ft) tall
Key features
Similar to honeysuckle but a small shrub, with paired yellowish cream flowers 8–15mm (⅜–⅝in) long and bright red berries
Flowering time
May–June

● **Ivy**
Hedera helix
Habitat and distribution
Woods, hedgerows, cliffs and gardens on all but very wet or acid soils
Size Up to 30m (100ft) tall
Key features
Creeping and climbing woody stemmed evergreen, attaches by tiny roots; leaves glossy, 3 or 5-lobed or pointed oval; flowers green with yellow anthers, in erect umbels (umbrella-like clusters); berries black
Flowering time
September–November

● **Sea bindweed**
Calystegia soldanella
Habitat and distribution
Widespread but local on sand dunes or shingle beaches; climbs up marram grass in western Ireland; absent from north-eastern Scotland
Size 5–30cm (2–12in) tall
Key features
Creeping or twining perennial; small, round, fleshy leaves; flowers solitary, 35–50mm (1⅜–2in) across, pink with fine white stripes, and a pair of sepal-like bracts at the base; fruit a 2-celled capsule
Flowering time
June–August

● **Black bryony**
Tamus communis
Habitat and distribution
Widespread in hedges and scrub and woodland in southern England and Wales; in Ireland only Co. Sligo
Size 1–4m (3–13ft) tall
Key features
Hairless perennial, with yam-like tuber; leaves heart-shaped, pointed, shiny, tiny flowers 3–6mm (⅛–¼in) across, male and female on separate plants, 6 petals, greenish yellow in long clusters; fruit a loose cluster of very poisonous shiny red berries
Flowering time
May–September

● **White bryony**
Bryonia dioica
Habitat and distribution
Widespread in hedges and scrub, mostly in southern half of England but not in south-west; introduced in Ireland, near Dublin
Size 1–4m (3–13ft) tall
Key features
Rough hairy perennial, with a stout tuber; leaves ivy-like, 5 or 7-lobed, with a coiled tendril opposite each; male and female flowers on separate plants, 5 petals, greenish white with darker veins; fruit a cluster of very poisonous red berries
Flowering time
May–September

● **Honeysuckle or woodbine**
Lonicera periclymenum
Habitat and distribution Common in hedges, woodland and coastal heaths and cliffs
Size 2–6m (6½–20ft) tall
Key features
Woody perennial; leaves in opposite pairs, oval, slightly paler beneath; flowers in flat clusters, 40–50mm (1½–2in) long, tubular, 2-lipped, yellowish cream (deepening to orange-buff after pollination) tinged with lilac or crimson; fragrant, shiny red berries
Flowering time
June–September

Large bindweed or American bellbine
Calystegia silvatica

Honeysuckle
Lonicera periclymenum

Sea bindweed
Calystegia soldanella

White bryony
Bryonia dioica

Black bryony
Tamus communis

Ivy
Hedera helix

Fly honeysuckle
Lonicera xylosteum

► Although sea bindweed is a true climber, it is more often seen creeping along the ground since it grows on almost bare coastal shingle.

▼ Clusters of hops in an autumn hedgerow are a familiar sight throughout much of lowland Britain, although widespread planting gives a false impression of its natural range.

▼ The delicate flowers of fly honeysuckle are a very rare sight, confined to a few woods on the South Downs. The flowers appear in May and June and, despite their relatively small size, are pollinated mainly by bumblebees.

WILDLIFE WATCH

Where can I see climbing plants?

● Hedges and woodland margins are good places to look for climbing plants.

● Many climbers and scramblers are at their best in late summer and autumn, when the fruits are conspicuous. The feathery fruits of traveller's joy festoon hedges and woods on chalk and limestone in autumn and winter.

● Field bindweed and black-bindweed prefer disturbed ground. Some climbers, such as hop that has escaped from cultivation and large bindweed, grow on waste ground and alongside rivers and canals in urban areas.

Index

Page numbers in *italic* refer to the illustrations

A

admiral butterflies
 red 26, *26*
 white *6*
anemone, wood *30*, 31, 33, 36
ants 7
 blood-red (*Formica sanguinea*) 109–10, *109–10*
 Formica fusca 109
 Formica rubifarbis 109
 Strongylognathus testaceus 110
 turf (*Tetramorium caespitum*) 110
 wood (*Formica rufa*) 109
aphids 17
apple (*Malus domestica*) 22–27, *22–27*
 crab (*Malus sylvestris*) 22, 23, *23*, 28, *30*
arable farmland 12–17, *12–17*
ash trees 30, 34, 111
aspen (*Populus tremula*) *112*, 114, *114*

B

badger 27
barley *14*
bat, long-eared *6*
beans, field 12
beech trees 34, 36, *36*, 111
bees 20, 24–25
beetle banks 17
bellbine (*Calystegia sepium*) 123, *123*
 American (*Calystegia silvatica*) 124, *124*
bindweeds 121
 black (*Fallopia convolvulus*) 122, 123, *123*
 copse (*Fallopia dumetorum*) 122, 123, *123*
 field (*Convolvulus arvensis*) 122, 123, *123*
 hedge (*Calystegia sepium*) 121, 122, *122*, 123, *123*
 large (*Calystegia silvatica*) 122, 124, *124*
 sea (*Calystegia soldanella*) 122, 124, *124*, *125*
birch, silver 111
birds
 in the Chilterns 34, 35
 in hazel coppices 32–33
 on roadside verges 21
 see also individual species
bird's-nest, yellow 36
bittercress 36
blackberry 9
blackbird 9, 26, 33
blackcap 9, 24, 33, 34
bluebell *20*, 32, 33, 36
blue butterflies
 Adonis (*Polyommatus bellargus*) 7, 66, *66*, 69, *69*
 chalkhill (*Polyommatus coridon*) 35, 66, 69, *69*
 common (*Polyommatus icarus*) 35, 66, 69, *69*
 small (*Cupido minimus*) 68, *68*
brambles 9, 18, 20, 32, 33
brimstone butterfly *32*, 33
brown argus butterfly (*Agricia agrestis*) 35, 66, 68, *68*

bryonies 121
 black (*Tamus communis*) 121, 122, 124, *124*
 white (*Bryonia dioica*) 122, 124, *124*
bugle 31, *31*, 32
bullfinch (*Pyrrhula pyrrhula*) 9, 24, *24*, 98–101, *98–101*
bullhead 35
buntings
 cirl 15, *15*, 26, *26*
 corn 15, *15*, 35
 Lapland 56
 reed 14
 snow 56
burnet, salad 24, 35, 36
burnet moths 64–65
 five-spot 65, *65*
 narrow-bordered five-spot 65, *65*
 New Forest 65
 Scotch 65
 six-spot *64*, 65, *65*
 slender Scotch 65
 transparent 65
bush crickets 20
 great green 20
 Roesel's 18, *18*
buttercup, meadow 24
butterflies
 in apple orchards 25
 in the Chilterns 34, 35
 downland butterflies 7, 66–70, *66–70*
 in hazel coppices 32
 on roadside verges 20
 woodland butterflies 9
 see also individual types of butterfly
buzzard 18, 35

C

calamint, lesser 19
campions
 red *20*, 32
 white 20
candytuft, wild 36, *36*
capsid bug, black-kneed 26
carrots 14
catkins, hazel 29, *29*, 30
celandine, greater (*Chelidonium majus*) 74, *74*, 77, *77*
centaury, common 36
chaffinch 34
chalk downland, Chilterns 34–37, *34–37*
cherry trees
 bird (*Prunus padus*) *112*, 114, *114*
 wild 28, *30*
chiffchaff (*Phylloscopus collybita*) 32, *33*, 102, 103, *103*
Chilterns 34–37, *34–37*
chukar 16
cinnabar moth 7
climbing plants 121–5, *121–5*
clovers 8, 35, 78–82
 alsike ((*Trifolium hybridum*) 79, *79*
 bird's-foot (*Trifolium ornithopodioides*) 79, *79*
 burrowing or subterranean (*Trifolium subterraneum*) 79, *79*
 clustered (*Trifolium glomeratum*) 81, *81*
 crimson (*Trifolium incarnatum* subsp. *incarnatum*) 80, *80*
 hare's-foot (*Trifolium arvense*) 82, *82*

knotted (*Trifolium striatum*) 81, *81*
 long-headed (*Trifolium incarnatum* subsp. *molinerii*) 80, *80*
 red (*Trifolium pratense*) 24, 78, 80, *80*
 reversed (*Trifolium resupinatum*) 80
 rough (*Trifolium scabrum*) 81, *81*
 sea (*Trifolium squamosum*) 82, *82*
 starry (*Trifolium stellatum*) 82, *82*
 strawberry (*Trifolium fragiferum*) 80, *80*
 suckling (*Trifolium dubium*) 81, *81*
 suffocated (*Trifolium suffocatum*) 82, *82*
 sulphur (*Trifolium ochroleucon*) 80, *80*
 twin-headed (*Trifolium bocconei*) 82, *82*
 upright (*Trifolium strictum*) 82, *82*
 western (*Trifolium occidentale*) 79, *79*
 white or Dutch (*Trifolium repens*) 78, *78*, 79, *79*
 zigzag (*Trifolium medium*) 80, *80*
comma butterfly 26, *26*
'conservation headlands' 14, 17
coppices, hazel 9, 28–33, *28–33*
coralroot 36
corncockle *17*, 19
corncrake (*Crex crex*) *7*, 8
cornflower 8, *12*, 13, 19
Countryside Stewardship scheme 17
cowslip 19, 24, *24*, 36
crayfish, white-clawed 35
crow 17, 21
cudweed, red-tipped 19
curlew, stone 15, *15*

D

dace 35
daffodil 31, *31*, 33
daisies 19
 ox-eye *6*, *19*, 20, 24
dandelion *12*, 19
deer 32, 33
 fallow 84
 muntjac 26–27
 red 84
 roe (*Capreolus capreolus*) 9, 26–27, *33*, 84–89, *84–89*
dormouse
 common (*Muscardinus avellanarius*) 9, 30, *32*, 33, 90–93, *90–93*
 fat (edible) 35, *35*
downland, Chilterns 34–37, *34–37*
dropwort 36
dunnock 33

E

Environmentally Sensitive Areas (ESAs) 17
eyebright 35

F

farmland, arable 12–17, *12–17*
felwort 36
fenugreek (*Trifolium ornithopodioides*) 79, *79*
fertilisers, arable farming 13
fieldfare 26
firecrest (*Regulus ignicapillus*) 102, 104, *104*
fish, in the Chilterns 35
flowers *see* plants

flycatcher
 pied *8*, 9
 spotted 34
forget-me-nots 116–20
 Alpine (*Myosotis alpestris*) 116, 118, *118*, *119*
 changing or yellow and blue (*Myosotis discolor*) 120, *120*
 creeping (*Myosotis secunda*) 118, *119*
 early (*Myosotis ramosissima*) *117*, 120, *120*
 field (*Myosotis arvensis*) 116, 120, *120*
 Jersey (*Myosotis sicula*) 116, 118, *119*
 pale (*Myosotis stolonifera*) 118, *118*
 tufted (*Myosotis laxa*) 118, *119*
 water (*Myosotis scorpioides*) 118, *118*
 wood (*Myosotis sylvatica*) 116, *117*, 118, *119*
fox 9, 16, *16*, 18, 20, *20*, 27
foxglove 19, 31, 33
fox hunting 13–14, 16
fritillary butterflies 33
 dark green (*Argynnis aglaja*) 35, 68, *68*
 Duke of Burgundy 35
 pearl-bordered 32
 silver-washed 9, 32, *32*
frogs 21
fruit, apple orchards 22–27, *22–27*

G

garlic, wild *20*
gean *see* cherry, wild
gentians 35
 autumn *see* felwort
 Chiltern 36, *36*
 early 36
 fringed 36
glow-worms
 Lampyris noctiluca 71–72, *71–72*
 Phosphaenus hemipterus 72
goldcrest (*Regulus regulus*) 102, 104, *104*
goldfinch 20
gorse 20–21
grasshoppers *6*, *17*
grasslands, chalk 34–35, 36
grayling 35
grebe, little 14
ground beetles *17*
ground-pine 37
guelder rose 28, *30*
gulls 14, *14*
 black-headed *14*
 common *14*
 herring *14*

H

hare, brown *13*, 16, *24*
hawfinch *9*
hay 8
hazel (*Corylus avellana*) 9, 28–33, *28–33*, 111, *112*, 113, *113*
heath butterfly, small 35
hedgehog 21, *26*, 27
hellebore, green 36
helleborine
 narrow-lipped 36
 red 36
herb-Paris 32
hobby 14

honeysuckles 121, *121*, 122
    fly (*Lonicera xylosteum*) 122, 124, *124*, *125*
    Lonicera periclymenum 124, *124*
hop (*Humulus lupulus*) 121, 122, 123, *123*, *125*
horned-poppies 73
    red (*Glaucium corniculatum*) 75, *75*
    yellow (*Glaucium flavum*) 74, 75, *75*
hounds-tongue, green 19
hoverflies 9, 20, 25
hunting 13–14, 16

I
insecticides 13
insects
    in apple orchards 24–26
    in the Chilterns 34, 35
    in hazel coppices 32–33
    on roadside verges 20
    see also individual types of insect
iris, yellow 35
ivy (*Hedera helix*) 121, 122, 124, *124*

K
kestrel 14, *19*, 20, 35
kite, red 35, *35*

L
lapwing (*Vanellus vanellus*) 8, *12*, 14, 58–63, *58–63*
lark, shore 56, *56*
leeks 12
lime trees 24
linseed 12

M
machair 7–8
magpie *21*
maize 12, 14
mallard 14
mangels 14
maple, field (*Acer campestre*) 111, *112*, 113, *113*
marbled white butterfly (*Melanargia galathea*) *19*, 35, 66, 67, *67*
marigold, corn 12, *18*, 19
mayweed 8
meadow brown butterfly (*Maniola jurtina*) 20, 66, *66*, 67, *67*
meadows, in orchards 24
mercury, dog's 31
mezereon 36
mice
    harvest *12*
    wood 9, *9*, 27
    yellow-necked 32, *32*
mignonette 36
milkwort 36
mistletoe 24, *25*
mole *8*
mountain ash (*Sorbus aucuparia*) 111, *111*, *112*, 115, *115*
mullein, white 19

N
newts 21
nightingale 33, *33*
nuthatch 34

O
oak trees 30, 34
    pedunculate 111
    sessile 111
oats 14
oilseed rape 12
old man's beard (*Clematis vitalba*) 123, *123*
orange-tip butterfly 34
orchards, apple 22–27, *22–27*
orchids 6, 7, 33, 35
    bee 6, *9*, *18*, 36
    common spotted 24, *24*, 36
    early purple 24, *30*, 32
    fragrant 36
    ghost 36, *36*
    marsh 35
    military 36, *36*
    musk 36
    pyramidal 6, 36
    spotted 19, *19*
owls 21
    barn 14, *17*, 21
    little 14, 21
    short-eared 35
    tawny *20*

P
painted lady butterfly 19–20
pansy, field 13
parasol mushroom *7*
partridges 14
    grey 16, *16*
    red-legged 16, *16*
pasqueflower 36
peas 12, 14
pesticides 15
pheasant 14, 16, *16*, 21
pheasant's-eye 37
pimpernel, yellow 31, *31*
pipit, meadow 12, 14, 35
plants
    in the Chilterns 34–35, 36
    in hazel coppices 31, 32
    on roadside verges 18–20
    see also individual types of plant
plovers
    American golden (*Pluvialis dominica*) 60
    golden (*Pluvialis apricaria*) *17*, 60, *60*
    green *see* lapwing
    Pacific golden (*Pluvialis fulvia*) 60
poplars 24
    black (*Populus nigra*) *112*, 113, *113*
poppies 8, 12–13, *12*, *13*, *18*, 19, 73–77, *73*, *74*
    Atlas or Atlantic (*Papaver atlanticum*) 77, *77*
    Babington's (*Papaver dubium* subsp. *lecoqii*) 76, 77
    Californian (*Eschscholzia californica*) 76, 77
    common (*Papaver rhoeas*) 74, *76*, 77
    long-headed (*Papaver dubium* subsp. *dubium*) 74, *76*, 77
    opium (*Papaver somniferum*) 74, *74*, *77*, 77
    prickly (*Papaver argemone*) 74, *76*, 77
    rough (*Papaver hybridum*) 74, *76*, 77
    shirley 74
    Welsh (*Meconopsis cambrica*) 75, *75*

potatoes 12, 14
primrose 24, 31, 33
purple emperor butterfly 9, 105–6, *105–6*

R
rabbit *20*
ragwort 7, *19*, 20
rampion, spiked 19
ramsons *20*
rattle, yellow 24, 36
red spider mite 25–26
redstart (*Phoenicurus phoenicurus*) 9, 94–97, *94–97*
    black 97, *97*
redwing 26
ringlet butterfly 20
roadside verges 18–21, *18–21*
robin 33
rook 21
rowan (*Sorbus aucuparia*) 111, *111*, *112*, 115, *115*
rye 14

S
scabious, field 36
scrambling plants 121–5, *121–5*
scurvygrass, common 19
set-aside scheme 17
shooting 13–14, 16
shrews
    common (*Sorex araneus*) 40–45, *40–45*
    pygmy 40, 45
    water 40, 45
silverweed 7
skipper butterflies
    dingy (*Erynnis tages*) 35, 70, *70*
    grizzled (*Pyrgus malvae*) 35, 70, *70*
    silver-spotted (*Hesperia comma*) 35, 66, 70, *70*
skylark (*Alauda arvensis*) 8, *12*, 14, *17*, 35, 52–57, *52–57*
slug, lemon *36*
Solomon's seal 32
sorrel, wood 31
speckled wood butterfly 9, 32, 33, 34
speedwells 7
spurge-laurel 36
squirrel, grey 9, *29*, 32, 33
stag beetle 107–8, *107–8*
sticklebacks 35
stitchwort, greater 31, 36
streams, in the Chilterns 35–37
stubble fields 13, 15
sugar beet 12, 14
sweet vernal grass 6
sycamore (*Acer pseudoplatanus*) *112*, 114, *114*

T
teasel 19, 20
thistle, spear 19, 20
thrushes 9, 24, 32, 33
    mistle 24, *25*
    song 26
thyme, wild 34
tits 32, 34
    blue 24, 25
toad 21, *21*
tortoiseshell butterfly 26
traveller's joy (*Clematis vitalba*) 121, 122, *122*, 123, *123*

treecreeper 9, *25*, 26
trees
    apple orchards 22–27, *22–27*
    hazel coppices 9, 28–33, *28–33*
    smaller deciduous trees 111–16, *111–16*
    see also individual types of tree
trefoils 7, 35
    hop (*Trifolium campestre*) 81, *81*
    large or large hop (*Trifolium aureum*) 81, *81*
    lesser (*Trifolium dubium*) 81, *81*
    slender (*Trifolium micranthum*) 81, *81*
    soft (*Trifolium scabrum*) 81, *81*
trout, brown 35
turnips 12, 14, *14*

V
verges, roadside 18–21, *18–21*
vetches 7, 35
    horseshoe 7, 36
    kidney 36
violets 33
    dog 32
    marsh 32
voles
    field (*Microtus agrestis*) *19*, 20, 46–51, *46–51*
    Orkney (*Microtus arvalis orcadensis*) 50, *50*

W
warblers 32, 33, 102–4
    garden *33*
    willow (*Phylloscopus trochilus*) 8, 32, 33, 102, *102*, 103, *103*
    wood (*Phylloscopus sibilatrix*) 34, 102, 104, *104*
wasps 25, 26
watercress 35, 37
water-crowfoot 35
wheat 13, 14
whitebeam, common (*Sorbus aria*) *112*, 115, *115*
white butterflies
    green-veined 32, 33, 34
    small *17*
whitethroat 8, 9
wild service tree (*Sorbus torminalis*) 111, *112*, 115, *115*
willowherb, rosebay 21
windflower *see* anemone, wood
winter moth 25
woodbine (*Lonicera periclymenum*) 124, *124*
woodcock 34
woodlands
    Chilterns 34
    hazel coppices 28–33, *28–33*
woodlark (*Lullula arborea*) 56, *56*
woodpeckers
    great spotted 34
    green 34
woodpigeon 17
wren 33

Y
yarrow 24
yellowhammer 8, 35
yellow rattle *8*
yellow-wort 36

Photographs: Cover ardea.com/Steve Hopkin, inset WW/Steve Austin, back cover FLPA/J. Hawkins; 1 NP/F. Blackburn; 2-3 WW; 4 WP/D. Tipling; 5(t) NP, (b) NP; 6(bl) BC/K.Taylor, (bc) NP/P.Sterry, (br) NP/A.Cleave; 7(bl) NP/P.Sterry, (bc) NP/P.Sterry, (br) NP/P.Sterry; 8(bl) NP/H.Clark, (br) NP/P.Sterry; 9(bl) NP/P.Sterry, (bc) NP/R.Tidman, (br) NP; 10-11 WW; 12(sp,bl,bc,bru) NP; 13(br) NP; 14(tl) NP, (tr,cru,cr) GWM, (c) NP; 15(b) NP, (tr) FLPA/John Hawkins, (cr,cl) NP; 16(tr,c) FLPA, (bl,bcu) NP; 17(tr,cr,bl,bc,sp) NP; 18(tr) FLPA/T.Wharton, (br) NP/P.Sterry, (b) Ardea/J.Bottomley; 19(tl) NP/T.Wharton, (tc) NP/P.Green, (tr) NP/P.Newman, (bl) David Chapman, (br) NP/E.A.Janes; 20(tl) NP/R.Mearns, (cl) FLPA/T.Whittaker, (cr) Ardea/M.Watson, (br) Ardea/B.Gibbons; 21(tl) BC/G.McCarthy, (tr) FLPA/R.Chiltenden, (bl) Ardea; 22(b) Corbis/Paul.A Souders; 23(b) NP/P.Sterry; 24(tl) NP/P.Sterry, (cr) FLPA/A.R Hamblin, (bl) FLPA/N.Nimmo, (bc) NP/P.Sterry; 25(tl) BC/J.Burton, (tc) NP/J.Hall, (tr) NP/C.Carver, (b) NHPA/J.Gifford; 26(tr) WP/J.Roberts, (blu) Ardea/Tom Bomford, (br) NHPA/M.Garwood, (bc) BC/W.S Paton; 27(b) NP/S.C.Bisserot; 28(b) English Nature/Paul Glendell; 29(bl) NP/P.Sterry, (br) NP/P.Sterry; 30(tl,tl,tr,cru,c,bc) NP;31 NP; 32 NP; 33(tl,tc,tr) NP, (c) Ardea/Andrew Darrington; 34(b) NP/R.Bush; 35(cr) Mike Read, (bru) NP/R.Bush; 36(tl,tc,tr,cl,br) NP, (bl) NV/H.Angel; 40(br) NPL/Jim Hallett; 41(tr) BC/Jane Burton, (b) BC/Dr.P Evans; 40-41 ardea.com/Chris Knights; 42(tr) FLPA, (cr) NP/Owen Newman; 43(tr) BC, (cl) AQ; 44(tr) Ardea/P.Morris, (cr) FLPA; 45(tr) FLPA/E&D Hosking, (cr) BC/Colin Varndell; 46(b) FLPA/E.Hosking; 47(tr) WW/J.Robinson, (b) RSPCA/C.Carver; 48(tr) NPL/B.Lightfoot, (bl)Ardea/J.Beams, (br) WW/S.Austin; 49(tl) NV/H.Angel, (tr) RSPCA/C.Carver; 50(tl) NP/P.Sterry, (tr) WW/S.Austin, (bl) BC/J.Markham, (br) NHPA/H&V Incien; 51(tl) PEP/P.Chippendale, (bl) Ardea/A.Lindau; 52(c) FLPA/J.Hawkins; 53(tr) NHPA/W.Murray, (b) AQ/M.Lane; 54(tl) FLPA/J.Hawkins, (tc) FLPA/M.Jones, (tr) NPL/D.Nill, (cl) AQ/H.Gobius, (c) NHPA/M.Lane, (cr) AQ/N.Ede; 55(tr) WP/D.Tipling, (bl) BC/B.Glover; 56(tr) FLPA/S,D&K Maslows, (cl) FLPA/H.Clark, (cr) NHPA/M.Grey, (bl) Ardea/R.Smith; 57(tr) WP/D.Tipling, (cr) FLPA/R.Wilmhurst (bl) NP/K.Carlson; 58(b) NHPA/Paal Hermansen; 59(tr) BC/J.Cancalosis, (b) Ardea/C&J Knights; 60(tr) FLPA/J.Baks, (cl) BC/A.G Potts, (c) BC/K.Taylor, (b) FLPA/W.Wisniewski; 61(cl) BC/R.Glover, (c) OSF/D.Thompson, (cr) NP/R.Tidman, (bl) BC/R.Glover, (bc) Ardea/J.P Ferrero, (br) OSF/W.Paton; 62(tr) Ardea/C.Knights, (cl) FLPA/E&D Hosking, (bl) BC/E.Pott, (br) BC/G.Lansbury; 63(tc) BC/W.S Paton, (cl) FLPA/P.Moore; 64(r) NHPA/S.Dalton, (bl) NV/H.Angel; 65(tlu) FLPA/P.Haynes, (tr) NP/L.Jessup, (tl) NP/J.Hall, (bc) PW/K.G Preston Mafham; 66(cr,bru) PW; 67(tr) PW, (cl) NPL/George McCarth, (bl) PW/K.G Preston Mafham; 68(tl) NPL/George McCarth, (cl,bl) PW; 69(tl) NPL/David Kjaer, (cl) NHPA/Alan Barnes, (bl) FLPA/Chris Newton; 70(tl,cl) PW, (bl) NPL/George McCarth; 71(cr) NV/H.Angel, (bc) NI, (bl) NP/P.Sterry; 72(tr) NP/P.Sterry, (cr) FLPA/H.Clark, (bl) NP/P.Sterry; 73(b) NV/H.Angel; 74(tl) NV/H.Angel, (c) FLPA/M.J.Thomas, (tr) OSF/Erica Lennard, (bc) NHPA/Ernie Janes; 78(bl) NP/P.Sterry, (br) Andrew Gagg; 80(bl) NI/B.Gibbons; 82(tr) NV/H.Angel; 83 WW/Alastair G. Baker; 84(c) Andy Rouse; 85(tr) NHPA, (b) Andy Rouse; 86(tr) NHPA/M.Danegger; 87(tr) NHPA/M.Danegger, (cl) AQ/R.Seigal; 88(tr) NHPA/Danegger, (bc) NHPA/M.Danegger; 89(tl) FLPA/G.Laci, (tr) NHPA/M.Danegger, (b) FLPA/R.Bender; 90(bl) NP/Owen Newman; 91(tl) NP/Owen Newman, (cr) NP/Owen Newman, (br) NP/Owen Newman; 92(t) NP/Owen Newman, (br) NP/Owen Newman; 93(tc) NP/Owen Newman, (b) BC/Jane Burton; 94(br) FLPA/H.Clark; 95(tr) Ardea/B.Bevan, (c) NHPA/A.Williams, (br) Mike Read; 96(tl,tc) Mike Read, (tr) WW/M.Powles, (cl) NP/H.Clark, (c) OSF/D.Tipling; 97(tl) OSF/M.Birkhead, (tr) OSF/C.Sanchez, (bl) FLPA/R.Wilmhurst; 98(tr) BC/K.Taylor, (b) FLPA/J.Hawkins; 99(tr) BC/K.Taylor, (c) BC/U.Walz, (br) BC/J.Jurka; 100(bl) FLPA/T.Hamblin, (br) FLPA/G.Andrewartha; 101(tc) FLPA/R.Wilmhurst, (tr) AQ/P.T Castell, (c) FLPA/R.Wilmhurst, (cr) AQ/R.Siegel, (bl) FLPA/A.Wharton; 102(cr) WP/D.Mason; 103(cl) AQ/M.C Wilkes, (bl) FLPA/R.Brooks; 104(tl) WP/R.Brooks, (cl) NP/P.Sterry, (bl) WP/D.Tipling; 105 (tr) FLPA/H.Clark, (bl) OSF/K.Porter, (bc) FLPA/ E&D Hosking, (br) OSF/ J.S&E.J Woolme; 106(tr) NP/F.Blackburn, (cr) NP/F.Blackburn, (bl) OSF/J.S&E.J Woolme; 107(l) NP/P.Sterry, (br) NP/R.Bush; 108(tr) NI/A.S.Harmer, (cl) NI/D.Elament, (c) Michael Chinery, (br) NP/S.C.Bisserot; 109(tr) R&C Foord, (bl) SPL/C.Nuridssany/M.Perennou, (br) R&C Foord; 110(tr) SPL/C.Nuridssany/M.Perennou, 111(bl) NV/H.Angel; 112(bl) NV/H.Angel; 113(tl,cl) NP, (bl) NV/H.Angel; 114(tl) NV/H.Angel, (cl) NP/E.A Janes, (bl) FLPA/E&D Hosking; 115(tl) NV/H.Angel, (bl) NP/E.A Janes; 116(t) NSc/R.Revels; 117(sp) NP/J.Hall, (tr) NSc/J.M&F.J Smith; 118(bl) NV/H.Angel; 121(b) BC/H.Reinhard; 122(tl) NV/H.Angel, (br) BC/ J.Van De Kam; 125(tl) NI, (tr) OSF/B.E.Watts, (bl) NP.

Illustrations: 23(t) Tim Hayward; 29(t) Ian Garrard; 42(b) John Ridyard; 49(b) John Ridyard; 54(b) John Ridyard; 61(tr) John Ridyard; 63(b) John Ridyard; 67-70(sp) Ian Garrard; 75-77(sp) Ian Garrard; 79-82(sp) Ian Garrard; 86(b) John Ridyard; 96(b) John Ridyard; 100(t) John Ridyard;103(tl) Tim Hayward; 110(b) Clive Pritchard; 118(sp) Ian Garrard; 123(sp) Ian Garrard.

Key to Photo Library Abbreviations: AQ = Aquila, BC = Bruce Coleman Ltd, FLPA = Frank Lane Photo Agency, GPL = Garden Picture Library, GWM = Garden/Wildlife Matters, NHPA = Natural History Photo Agency, NI = Natural Image, NP = Nature Photographers, NPL = Nature Picture Library, NSc = Natural Science Photos, NV = Natural Visions, OSF = Oxford Scientific Films, PEP = Planet Earth Pictures, PW = Premaphotos Wildlife, SPL = Science Photo Library, WP = Windrush Photos, WW = Woodfall Wild Images.

Key to position abbreviations: b = bottom, bl = bottom left, blu = bottom left upper, br = bottom right, bru =bottom right upper, c = centre, cl = centre left, clu = centre left upper, cr = centre right, cru = centre right upper, cu = centre upper, l = left, r = right, sp = spread, t = top, tl = top left, tlu = top left upper, tr = top right, tru = top right upper.

Wildlife Watch
Grassland & Woodland in Summer

Published by the Reader's Digest Association Limited, 2006

The Reader's Digest Association Limited
11 Westferry Circus, Canary Wharf
London E14 4HE

Reprinted 2008

We are committed both to the quality of our products and the service we provide to our customers, so please do contact us on 08705 113366, or via our website at: www.readersdigest.co.uk

If you have any comments about the content of our books you can contact us at: gbeditorial@readersdigest.co.uk

® Reader's Digest, The Digest and the Pegasus logo are registered trademarks of The Reader's Digest Association, Inc., of Pleasantville, New York, USA

Reader's Digest General Books:
Editorial Director   Julian Browne
Art Director   Anne-Marie Bulat
Series Editor   Christine Noble
Project Editor   Lisa Thomas
Project Art Editor   Julie Bennett
Prepress Accounts Manager   Dean Russell

This book was designed, edited and produced by Eaglemoss Publications Ltd, based on material first published as the partwork *Wildlife of Britain*

For Eaglemoss:
Project Editor   Marion Paull
Editors   Paul Brewer, Celia Coyne, Samantha Gray, John Woodward
Art Editor   Phil Gibbs
Editorial Assistant   Helen Hawksfield
Consultant   Jonathan Elphick

Publishing Manager   Nina Hathway

Copyright © Eaglemoss Publications Ltd/Midsummer Books Ltd 2006

Printed and bound in Europe by Arvato Iberia

Concept Code: UK 0133/G/S
Book code: 630-011 UP0000-3
ISBN: 978 0 276 44059 5
Oracle code: 356200009H.00.24